TEMPLAR, ARIZONA.

2 - The Mob Goes Wild

By Spike.

www.TemplarAZ.com

WWW.IRONCIRCUS .COM

This volume collects the second chapter of Templar, Arizona.
More of the story is available at http://www.templaraz.com.

Write Spike: ironcircus@gmail.com
First Edition: July 2008.
Second Edition: March 2010.

ISBN: 978-0-9794080-1-4

Printed in Canada

OKAY. SO.
IT'S LIKE, THE SECOND YOU GET INTO THE ROOM, SHE'S TIMING YOU.
HOW LONG YOU TAKE T'SIT DOWN. HOW LONG Y'TALK TO HER.
SHE MAKES YOU, YANNO, DO LITTLE PUZZLES? LIKE, MIND GAMES OR WHATEVER.
AND THEN SHE TIMES THAT.
IT'S A SCIENCE.
AND THEN SHE'S GOT THESE CHARTS?
YOU'RE ON THEM.
SHE TAKES YOUR TIMES AN' SHE FINDS YOU.
TEMPLAR DAMAGE REPORT
TDR
AND SHE CAN JUST DO YOUR WHOLE LIFE RIGHT THERE.
THE ENERGY IS JUST, LIKE, TOTALLY INSANE.
I CAN GET YOU AN APPOINTMENT, CURIO.
I CAN DO IT.
SHE'S GONNA BE ON MY SHOW.
SHE IS SERIOUSLY THE BEST HOROLOGIST IN THE WHOLE CITY.
FLAT
SHINER
really. wow.

...
SO?
HM?
Y'KNOW WHAT, I AM NOT EVEN GONNA TALK TO YOU ANYMORE.
FUCK.
MY GUEST. CURIO. FOR TELEVISION.
FLATWORM
I THOUGHT YOU WEREN'T GONNA DO GUESTS FROM NOW ON.
YOU SAID NOBODY WATCHED UNLESS YOU DID NAKED DANCING.
...OKAY.
FREEFORM. NATURALIST. EURYTHMY.
AND "MONDAYS WITH TUESDAY" IS A CONSTANTLY EVOLVING PROJECT. CUNT.
GOD. SHIT YOURSELF ABOUT IT.
PEEEEL
I AM ONLY SAYING.
WHAT EVER.
AT LEAST I DO SOMETHING.

I DO THINGS!
LOOK HOW COMPLETELY PSYCHOTIC YOU GET.
YOU KNOW HOW RIGHT I AM.
OH MY GOD LIKE YOU EVEN NOTICE OTHER PEOPLE, TUESDAY!
I AM ABOUT OTHER PEOPLE, CURIO.
AND MAYBE IF YOU WEREN'T SO DESPERATE FOR APPROVAL, NO ONE WOULD NOTICE HOW BAD YOU SUCK ON THE FOLLOW-THROUGH. STAGGERING CONCEPT.
WHY DO YOU EVEN CARE.
REMEMBER YOUR FUNK BAND?
I AM SURE YOU DO NOT.
YOU QUIT TO BE A SCULPTRESS, WHICH WAS ONLY, LIKE, TOO HILARIOUS, BY THE WAY.
GETTING OFF YET?
YOU DIDN'T EVEN DO YOUR ESCORT LICENSE ALL THE WAY.
EVEN ANTOINETTE DID HERS. AND SHE IS BASICALLY AN INVERTEBRATE.

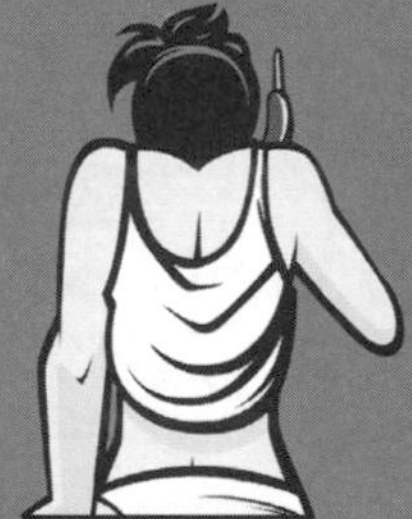

AND YOU WOULDN'T BE THIS GODDAMNED DEFENSIVE ANYWAY IF I WERE NOT TOTALLY CORRECT.

YEAH, 'M JUST SO FUCKIN' SURE, TUESDAY.

SEE, EXACTLY.

YOU DON'T LIKE WHAT I'VE GOT T'SAY, YOU JUST DON'T LIKE YOURSELF.

WHICH IS SO NOT MY PROBLEM. AND LIKE, BRUTALLY OBVIOUS.

DO ALL YOUR LOW PEOPLE FRIENDS KNOW YOU LIVE ON KING STREET?

SERIOUSLY FAKE, CURIO.

DO NOT.
YOU DO NOT CALL THEM THAT. EVER.
THEY CALL THEMSELVES THAT.
THEY DO NOT MEAN IT LIKE YOU MEAN IT.
REALLY.
HOW DO I MEAN IT?
ENLIGHTEN ME.
YOU KNOW HOW.
fft.
NO, TELL ME. SINCE YOU'RE SO IN TUNE WITH THE TERRIBLE SUFFERING OF THE DISENFRANCHISED UNDERCLASSES N'ALL.
SHIT, SHOULDN'T YOU BE DOWNSTAIRS, BLOCKIN' TRAFFIC WITH THE REST OF THE SOCIOECONOMIC AVANT-GARDE?
HMN?

JESUS CHRIST, CURIO.
LOOK OUT YOUR WINDOW.
LLLL

MY RHETORIC IS UNNECESSARY.
YOUR PRESENCE HERE TODAY IS PROOF.
YOUR DEDICATION RELIEVES ME OF MY RELEVANCE, AND THAT MAKES ME GLAD.
YOUR HEARTS AND MINDS HAVE EVOLVED BEYOND MY INSUFFICIENT POWERS OF PERSUASION.
YOU INDULGE ME, LIKE A RAMBLING GRANDPARENT.
I THANK YOU FOR THAT.
AND I THANK YOU BECAUSE YOU DO NOT ORATE.
ORATION IS IMPOTENT.
YOU SPEAK WITH HAMMERS.
AND YOU HAMMER BECAUSE THE BALLOT HAS FAILED.
THE MARKET HAS FAILED. THE LAW HAS FAILED.
SOCIETY IS POISONED BY ITS INEQUALITY.
TPD
IT REQUIRES A PURGE.
IT REQUIRES RECLAMATION.

KING STREET IS A MONUMENT TO THIS CITY'S GROTESQUE MISUSE OF ITS WEALTH.
AND ONE DAY, YOU WILL COME HERE AGAIN.
NOT TO RALLY. TO RECLAIM.
YOU SAW AND SOLDER AND BUILD UP THE ABANDONED RUINS OF SKINNER AND RIVERSIDE AND CHURCHYARD.
YOU TAKE THE BROKEN AND BOARDED-UP BUILDINGS AND YOU MAKE THEM WHOLE AND YOU SURRENDER THEM TO THE PEOPLE.
BUT YOU CAN NOT BE SATISFIED WITH STOCKYARDS AND FACTORIES.
RECLAMATION MUST CONTINUE. CHANGE MUST MATERIALIZE.
AND THIS?
THIS, THIS. THIS.
ALL OF IT.
THIS MUST NOT BE CONDONED.
IN A TEMPLAR WITH A SINGLE DESTITUTE CITIZEN, THIS MUST NOT BE TOLERATED.
YOU WILL TAKE DOWN THE TOWERS OF THE FEW AND MAKE THEM FIT FOR THE MANY.
REVOLUTION BEGINS IN THE HOMES OF THE PEOPLE.
AND YOU WILL BUILD THOSE HOMES.

HA!
HA HAH. OH, WOW.
WOW, I SO KNOW THAT FACE.
M'SORRY?

IT'S YOUR FIRST TIME HEARING BARNABAS JOHN IN PERSON, *RIGHT?*
YOU'VE GOT THAT LOOK.
I AM SO. **JEALOUS.**
I WISH IT COULD BE MY FIRST TIME **EVERY** TIME.
HM.
YANK.

I'M NUMBERS.
I'M BILL.
HI. BILL.
HI NUMBERS.
hee hee.
I'M WITH SOVIET NINE, OVER IN SKINNER. WE'RE RECLAIMING THE OLD CAPITAL TANNERY.
IT'LL FIT TEN FAMILIES, EASY.
WE'RE GONNA START TAKING TENANT APPLICATIONS IN FOUR MONTHS.
CITY PUBLIC HOUSING RESIDENTS ONLY.
ARE YOU WITH A SOVIET, YET?
MMNOPE.
BECAUSE YOU REALLY HAVE TO DO IT. HAVE TO.
IT IS SO SIGNIFICANT. IT'S INNOVATION.
UH HUH.
OKAY, FIRST OF ALL?
SELF-CONTAINED SEWAGE TREATMENT WITH GREY WATER RECYCLING. SOLAR POWER.
AQUAPONICS IN THE CELLAR.
SPINACH AND TILAPIA.
AND WE JUST MIXED ALL THE PAINT. DETOXIFYING COLORS. WARM PASTELS.

YOU CAN'T EVEN REALIZE WHAT ALL THAT MEANS.
WELL, NO, I GUESS YOU CAN. BUT YOU STILL CAN'T, RIGHT?
RIGHT, RIGHT.

IT'S EMANCIPATION FROM CAPITALIST EXPLOITATION.
FAIR PLAY.
THAT'S WHAT BARNABAS SAYS.

FIRST TIME I SAW HIM, HE WAS DOING THIS GUERILLA THING ON MY CAMPUS.
SECURITY GUYS WERE DRAGGING HIM OFF. HE WAS SCREAMING THAT. "FAIR PLAY."
EQUALITY.
AND THAT JUST HIT ME SO HARD. RECLAMATION IS IMPORTANT. IT NEEDS TO HAPPEN.
TOTALLY INSANE, HUH?

I REALLY WOULDN'T KNOW.

THERE ARE CRITICS WHO CLAIM YOUR ACTIONS ARE DISRUPTIVE.
THEY ARE CORRECT.
BUT IS IT THE DUTY OF A CONSCIENTIOUS REVOLUTIONARY TO.
TO DISRUPT THE.
ffFuck.
MISTER JOHN?
reclamation do not move.
do not stand and do not engage.
stay down stay with me.
this is not a challenge and this is not a defeat.
this serves no purpose and never intended to.

HUH.
WHAT'S GOIN' ON?
shhh.
PSSSHT.
BASH.
PSSHT.
BASH
TINKLE.

COFF
COUGH
COUGH
HACK
IT GOT ON ME!
IT GOT ON ME!!
PSSSHA
SHIT, IT'S BURNING!
WHAT?!
AAAA
NO IT IS NOT!
SHUTUP AND SIT DOWN!
COPS'R MOVIN'.
NO!
THIS IS REAL.
THIS IS REAL THIS IS REAL.
THE CAR'S FOUR BLOCKS DOWN.
STOP EVACUATING ME, JACKASSES!
THIS IS EXACTLY WHAT THEY WANT!
SNK. SNK. SNK.

THEY'RE COOK FAMILY!
AND YOU ARE FEEDING THE GOD DAMNED PANIC!
SSSSS.
SNK. SNK. SNK.
SNK. SNK.
SNI-THCHT
FOOMP.
ROAR.

TPD

TPD
DUSTIN.
TREASURE.
WE MUST INSIST UPON THE MERCY OF YOUR SILENCE.
JUDGEMENT SHALL NOW BE RENDERED.

WE HAVE HEARD BOTH SIDES OF THIS IMBROGLIO, AND WE MUST ADMIT TO A CERTAIN... INSTINCTUAL REVULSION.
IN THE COLISEUM
ARCHIVE - SE04 EP15
TREASURE IS COARSE. PLEBIAN. HER SPEECH IS GENEROUSLY TINGED WITH SCATOLOGICAL INVECTIVE.
THIS OFFENDS US.
HOWEVER, HER MANNER AND CARRIAGE ARE COURTLY ELEGANCE IN CONTRAST WITH DUSTIN'S LOUTISH OBLIQUITY.

HE HAS PERSISTED IN HIS DISHONESTY, DESPITE FULL KNOWLEDGE OF OUR INVESTIGATIVE ABILITIES.

HE HAS BEEN DUPLICITOUS ABOUT HIS INCOME. HIS PROPERTY. HIS PRE-EXISTING LEVELS OF DEBT.
WE DARE SAY HIS RELENTLESSLY BUFFOONISH ATTEMPTS AT SUBTERFUGE VERY NEARLY FORCED US TO RULE AGAINST TREASURE.
SCRUB SCRUB SCRUB.
WE BELIEVE SHE SHOULD BE PUNISHED FOR ISSUING THE OFFSPRING OF THIS CREATURE.

SCRATCH SCRATCH.
HOWEVER, IT MAY PLEASE HER TO KNOW WE LACK HER UNIQUELY MALICIOUS INSENSIBILITY.
THEREFORE, IN THE MATTER OF TREASURE DANIELS VERSUS DUSTIN FARBY.
DUSTIN.
OUR THUMB COMES DOWN.
AGAINST YOU.
WE RULE THAT TREASURE IS ENTITLED TO HALF OF YOUR PAY.
WE RULE THAT DUSTIN IS EVICTED FROM THE SHARED APARTMENT.
HOWEVER, WE REWARD NO ONE WITH THE STEREO SYSTEM.
IT SHALL BE SMASHED.
WE FIND IT VULGAR.
CLASS-INAPPROPRIATE. INTOLERABLE.
THE PICK-UP TRUCK SHALL LIKEWISE BE —
CLIC.
THUNDERBIRD TRIBE
VINLAND PEMMICAN
CLIC CLAC.

MUSS
COMB
RUMPLE.
CLUNK
SCCCCRAPE.
CLATTER.
THUMP.

FLUMP.

HEY.
HEY, KID.
RAP RAP.
NO.

LEMME IN, HUH?
NO AND GO AWAY.
C'MON.
NO! JUMP!
I'LL DIE.
OPEN THE WINDOW, PLEASE?

I'M DIALING. I'LL DO IT.
AH, HELL.
I WILL.
WHADDA YOU WANT, HUH?
I CAN'T GET BACK UP, I CAN'T GET DOWN.
I'M STUCK. BY ACCIDENT.
IF FUCKING WITH YOU WAS THE PLAN, I WOULDA USED THE DOOR.
Y'THINK I'M HERE TO KNOCK OUT THE WINDOW? FROM A LEDGE?
CRAWL IN THROUGH THE BROKEN GLASS? USE YOUR HEAD, ALREADY.

um.
YEAH, SEE. YOU KNOW IT'S DUMB.
uh.
WHY ARE YOU OUT THERE?

AH GOD DO NOT ASK ME THAT.
IT'S A GOD DAMNED EMBARASSMENT IS WHAT IT IS.
JUST SO UNPROFESSIONAL.
HEY, WHERE AM I?

I'M IN 2C.
NEIGHBORHOOD AND STREET.
OH, UH, THIS IS RIVERSIDE.
PAKHOM WAY.
THAT FAR?
huh.

HAVE YOU SEEN THE NEWS?
WHAT ARE THEY SAYING ABOUT KING STREET?
. . . I WAS WATCHING CARTOONS.
. . . right.

BEND DOWN.
WHAT?
I'M GONNA OPEN THE WINDOW. PUT YOUR HEAD DOWN.

OH. OKAY.
BUT YOU KNOW. I CAN'T REALLY LEAN OVER VERY–
BAM.

fffOW!! DAMN IT!
NO NO NO BACKWARDS LEAN BACK LEAN BACK LEAN BACK!

WHAP.

GUH.
UH.
OH. OH BOY I DID NOT MEAN THAT AT ALL I AM SO SORRY.
THE LATCH WAS.
it.
snf.

HLGHL.
NO, BREATHE IN. DEEP BREATHS.
YOU'LL ADJUST.
IS THAT THE KITCHEN?

WHY DO YOU SMELL LIKE DYING.
NIX ROUNDS.
CROWD SITUATION PERP MARKERS, INDELIBLE POLYMERIC PAINT PAYLOAD.
STANDARD RIOT GEAR.
THE STENCH IS NEW, THOUGH. AND I CAN'T RESPECT THAT.
THAT'S JUST THEM BEING DICKS.
THEM, *WHO?*
OH, COME ON.

D'YOU KNOW IF THERE'S A TRAIN LINE NEARBY?
BUS STOP? TAXI STAND? BIKESHARE?
ANYTHING?

THE UNDERGROUND'S FOUR BLOCKS SOUTH AND A RIGHT.
THAT'S PERFECT. THANKS.
EXCUSE ME, A FEW DAYS?
WHAT?
OH.
YEAH. A FEW. Y'KNOW, A COUPLE DAYS.
uhm. IT'S ON MY FACE, THOUGH.

NAH, IT'S COOL.
and my hand.
IF THE T.P. HASSLES YOU, SAY I POPPED YOU ONE. THEY'LL WANNA BELIEVE THAT.
HEY, WANT ME TO BREAK YOUR WINDOW? I KNOW HOW TO DO IT SO THE GLASS FALLS IN.

NO.
IT WOULDN'T BE ANY TROUBLE. LEAST I COULD DO.
PLEASE DON'T.
WELL, ALL RIGHT, THEN. YOUR DECISION.
TRAIL'S PROBABLY COLD BY NOW, ANYWAY.
YOU CAN SEE THE WINDOW FROM THE STREET, THOUGH, RIGHT?
UH HUH.
WHY?
STICK.
JUST CHECKING.

EPIPHANY?
DID YOU USE ALL OF THE MANGO-KIWI SCRUB?
IN THE LITTLE RED BOTTLE?
CUZ THAT'S JUST FOR YOUR *FACE*, NOT ALL OVER.
PLEASE DON'T DO THAT, OKAY? IT'S EXPENSIVE.
USE THE ALOE STUFF, THAT'S WHAT IT'S FOR.
PIPPI?
shhhk shhk shhhk.

SHRIEK!

RATTL!

WHO WUZ THAT *CHINEEZY* GUY?

WHAT?!

CUZ HE *LOOKED* AT ME AND YOU **NEED** T'DO SUMTHIN.

PIPPI GET OUT!

SO YOU DON'T **CARE.**

GET THE FUCK OUT RIGHT NOW OH MY GOD!

HMN.
WELL, THAT IS JUST SO REAL GOOD T'KNOW, HOW MUCH YOU GIVE A SHIT.
BOUNDARIES!

EPIPHANY, GET OUT OR I'M CALLING YOUR MOM!
GOD, SHUT UP.
PUT A LOCK ON MY DOOR? CUZ I AM UN CUMFTERBLE.

YOUR DOOR?
OUR DOOR. JESUS.
I WAS NOT WEARING PANTIES AN' HE LOOKED AT ME. HE LOOKED. AT ME.
AN' YOU CAN THINK I DO NOT CARE, BUT I AM SORRY CUZ I DO.
YOU CAN THINK WHATEVER THE FUCK YOU WANT AND I DO NOT CARE WHAT YOU HEARD.
I LIVE HERE AN' I DO WHAT I WANT WHERE I LIVE.

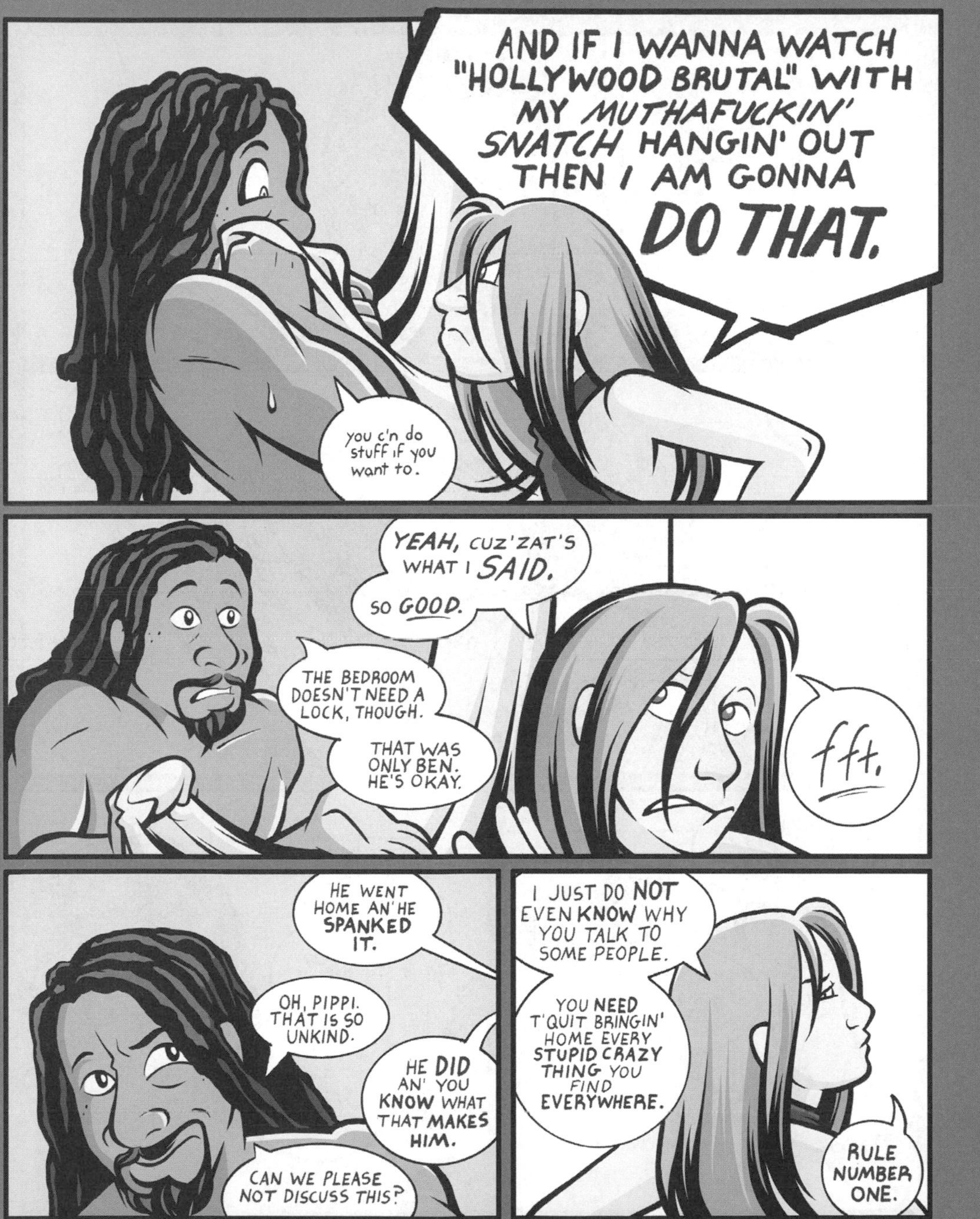

AND IF I WANNA WATCH "HOLLYWOOD BRUTAL" WITH MY *MUTHAFUCKIN'* *SNATCH* HANGIN' OUT THEN I AM GONNA **DO THAT.**

you c'n do stuff if you want to.

YEAH, CUZ'ZAT'S WHAT I *SAID*.
SO GOOD.
THE BEDROOM DOESN'T NEED A LOCK, THOUGH.
THAT WAS ONLY BEN. HE'S OKAY.
fft.

HE WENT HOME AN' HE **SPANKED IT.**
OH, PIPPI. THAT IS SO UNKIND.
HE **DID** AN' YOU **KNOW** WHAT THAT **MAKES HIM.**
CAN WE PLEASE NOT DISCUSS THIS?

I JUST DO **NOT** EVEN **KNOW** WHY YOU TALK TO SOME PEOPLE.
YOU **NEED** T'QUIT BRINGIN' HOME EVERY **STUPID CRAZY THING** YOU FIND **EVERYWHERE.**
RULE NUMBER ONE.

RIGHT. FINE.
AND THEN I NEED TO STOP DOING ALL OF YOUR HOMEWORK FOR YOU.
RULE NUMBER TWO.

NO YOU DON'T.
YES, I DO.
SCIP!!
WHAT.
SCIP, C'MON. C'MON C'MON COME ON.
NO, C'MON PLEASE?!
WE'VE HAD THIS CONVERSATION.

OH MY GOD COME ON!
YOU SAID YOU WERE GOING TO TRY THIS YEAR.
I CAAAN'T, IT'S TOO HARD! I'M STUPID!!

I WISH YOU WOULDN'T SAY THAT.
YOU HAFTA HELP ME!
NOBODY EVER HELPS ME,
OH MY GAHD!

THEY GONNA HOLD ME BACK AGAIN AN' YOU **KNOW** THEY ARE CUZ THEY *WANNA!!*

IT'S TH' MOST UNFAIR THING IN MY **WHOLE LIFE** AN' *NOBODY CARES!*

EPIPHANY, YOU WOULD PASS EVERY SINGLE COURSE IF YOU JUST **STUDIED.**

YOU DON'T EVEN GIVE IT A ***CHANCE.***

they put me in all th' dummy classes.

i'm embarrassed.

AW, PIPPI.

i dun' wanna go anymore.

EVER'BUDDY I KNOW'S A **YEAR AHEADA** ME.

THEY ALL MAKE **FUNNA** ME. I *KNOW* THEY DO.

uhm.

WELL... Y'MAYBE, UH... YOU WANNA JUST DO YOUR **G.E.D.?**

I MEAN, IT'S AN OPTION.

THAT TEST IS LIKE A **MILLION HOURS** *LONG.*

IT'S SHORTER THAN TWO MORE YEARS OF SCHOOL.

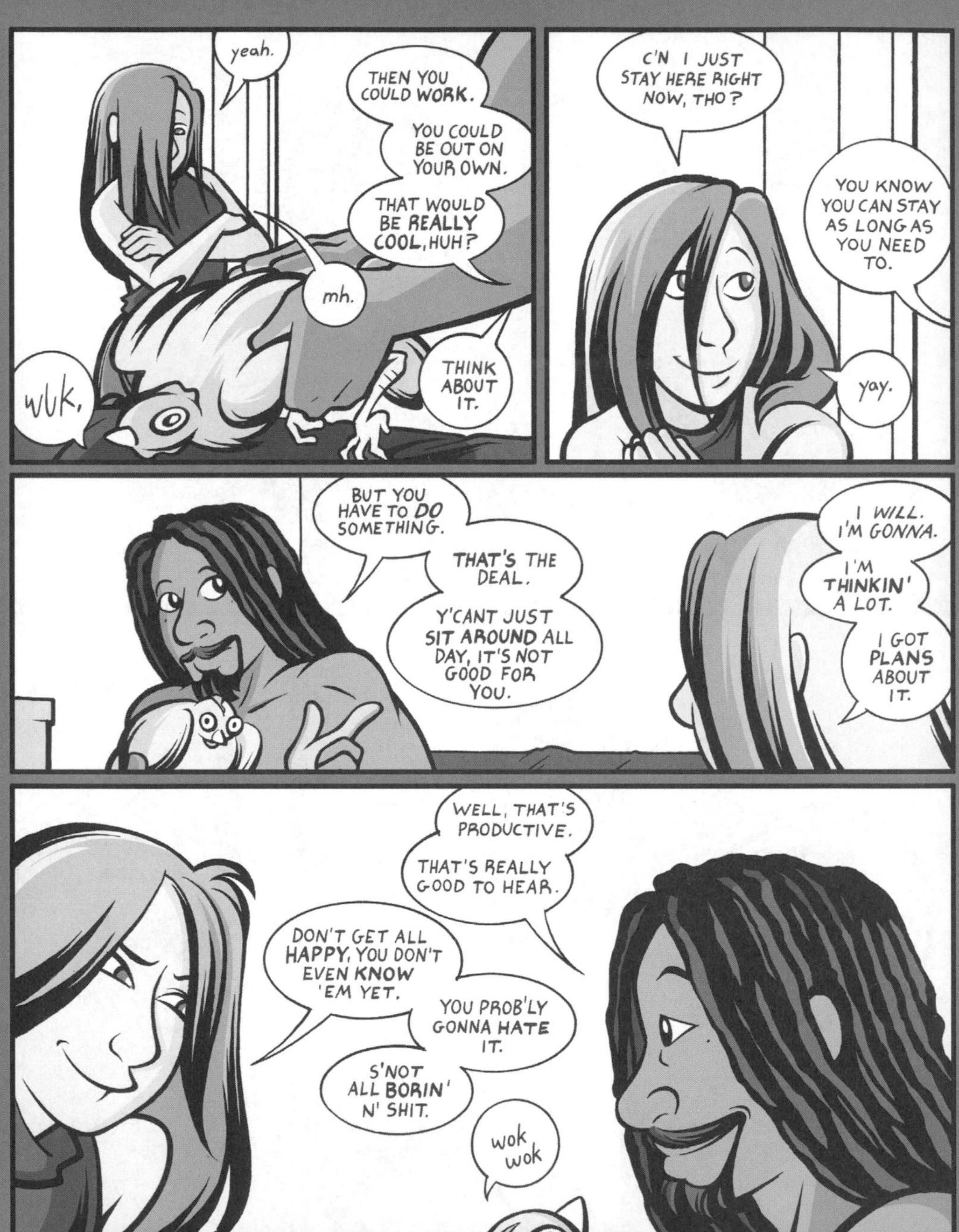
yeah.
THEN YOU COULD WORK.
YOU COULD BE OUT ON YOUR OWN.
THAT WOULD BE REALLY COOL, HUH?
mh.
WUK.
THINK ABOUT IT.
C'N I JUST STAY HERE RIGHT NOW, THO?
YOU KNOW YOU CAN STAY AS LONG AS YOU NEED TO.
yay.
BUT YOU HAVE TO DO SOMETHING.
THAT'S THE DEAL.
Y'CANT JUST SIT AROUND ALL DAY, IT'S NOT GOOD FOR YOU.
I WILL. I'M GONNA.
I'M THINKIN' A LOT.
I GOT PLANS ABOUT IT.
WELL, THAT'S PRODUCTIVE.
THAT'S REALLY GOOD TO HEAR.
DON'T GET ALL HAPPY, YOU DON'T EVEN KNOW 'EM YET.
YOU PROB'LY GONNA HATE IT.
S'NOT ALL BORIN' N' SHIT.
wok wok

I DUNNO. I'D FIGURE YOU WOULD WANT ALL THE **BORING** YOU COULD **GET**, THESE DAYS.

PSHT.

YOU WRONG ABOUT ***EVERYTHING.***

HAH.

baw.

I KNOW, I KNOW.

baahw.

ME, TOO.

FLORA.

HI, FLORA! HI, CHICKEN!

PRETTY CHICKEN.

HOWZAT WHOLE **CHICKEN** THING WORKIN' OUT FOR YA?

EVERYTHING OKAY?

PRETTY FLORA.

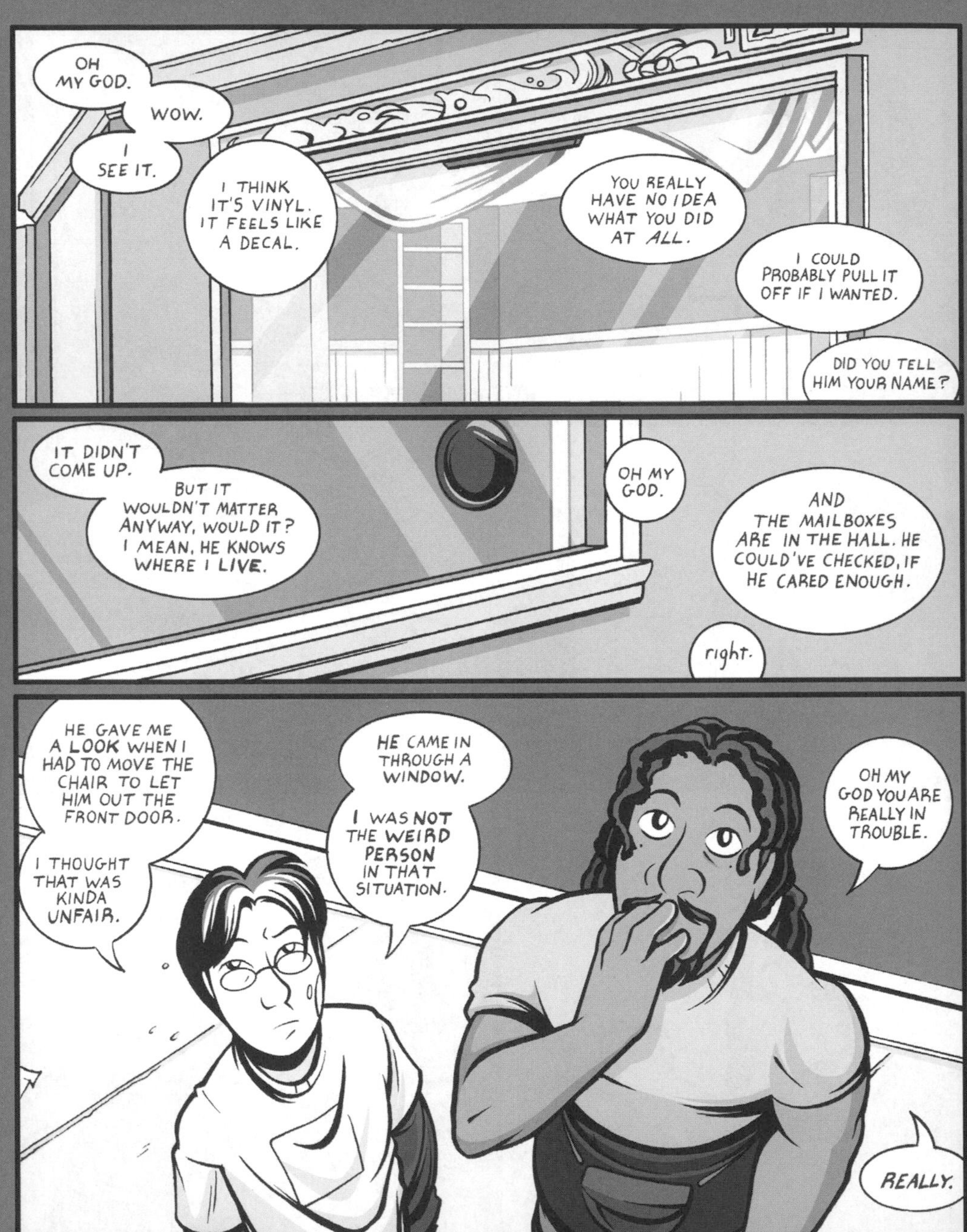
OH MY GOD.
WOW.
I SEE IT.
I THINK IT'S VINYL. IT FEELS LIKE A DECAL.
YOU REALLY HAVE NO IDEA WHAT YOU DID AT ALL.
I COULD PROBABLY PULL IT OFF IF I WANTED.
DID YOU TELL HIM YOUR NAME?
IT DIDN'T COME UP.
BUT IT WOULDN'T MATTER ANYWAY, WOULD IT? I MEAN, HE KNOWS WHERE I LIVE.
OH MY GOD.
AND THE MAILBOXES ARE IN THE HALL. HE COULD'VE CHECKED, IF HE CARED ENOUGH.
right.
HE GAVE ME A LOOK WHEN I HAD TO MOVE THE CHAIR TO LET HIM OUT THE FRONT DOOR.
I THOUGHT THAT WAS KINDA UNFAIR.
HE CAME IN THROUGH A WINDOW.
I WAS NOT THE WEIRD PERSON IN THAT SITUATION.
OH MY GOD YOU ARE REALLY IN TROUBLE.
REALLY.

I GUESS I MUST BE.
DOESN'T FEEL THAT WAY, THOUGH.
THAT GUY WAS A CRIMINAL. HE WAS IN YOUR HOUSE.
I KNOW, IT'S ODD. I'M NOT FREAKING OUT AT ALL.
I DUNNO.
I DUNNO, MAYBE YOU SHOULD STAY IN, T'DAY. PEOPLE WOULD UNDERSTAND.
THE PAINT AND EVERYTHING.
NAH, LET'S JUST GO.
IF THAT'S WHAT YOU WANT...
I KINDA WANNA SEE WHAT HAPPENS.
ARE YOU SERIOUS?
I THINK SO.
THAT'S COMPLETELY UNREASONABLE.
YOU'RE ORANGE.
I'VE GOT A STORY.
POW.
BUT YOU DON'T LOOK PUNCHED.
PUSHED, THEN.
TRIPPED OVER. GOOSED.
SOMETHING.

well, if you just wanna lie to people.
NOT EVERYONE. JUST POLICE.
IF THEY FIND ME.
WHICH THEY WON'T.

AND YOU'RE JUST GONNA LEAVE THAT STICKER WHERE IT IS, TOO.
I THINK I SHOULD.
AND YOU'RE SURE THAT'S SAFE.
NOT AT ALL.
NEW
THIS WEEK →
BEST SELLERS ☆
WORST S
AMBER'S CONFESSIONS

uh.
WHY DID YOU LET THAT GUY IN, AGAIN?
HE MADE A GOOD CASE. Y'KINDA HAD TO BE THERE.
I WOULD HAVE CALLED SOMEONE.

I ALMOST DID. I THREATENED TO, ANYWAY.
JUST LETTING HIM IN WAS EASIER.
oh.
HE WAS JUST A PROTESTER.
PROBABLY KICKED A BARRICADE OR SOMETHING.

JUST A PROTESTER.
WITH A GLUE-ON BEARD.
AND A WIG.
SURE, OKAY.

...
ARE YOU REALLY ALL RIGHT? CUZ YOU SEEM KINDA...
I DUNNO. BUZZED.
FOR YOU, I MEAN.
I FEEL GREAT.
I'M NOT SURE THAT YOU SHOULD.
MAYBE IT'S SHOCK.
UHM, DID YOU PASS OUT, AFTER?
IT'S NOT SHOCK.
IT'S RELIEF.

HMN.
WELL, YEAH. YEAH, I GUESS IT COULD HAVE BEEN WORSE.
THAT'S NOT HOW I MEAN IT.

YOU KNOW, I ALMOST DIDN'T MOVE HERE.
I GAVE UP ON IT FOUR TIMES BEFORE I LEFT THE HOUSE AND STAYED GONE.
WOW.
IT WASN'T BECAUSE OF THE CITY, THOUGH. IT WAS ME.
I COULD HAVE STAYED IN YAKIMA. I DIDN'T WANT TO.
BUT I DIDN'T WANT TO COME HERE AND HIT A WALL.
I DIDN'T WANT TO FIND OUT THE PROBLEM WASN'T GEOGRAPHY.
SURPRISE. I'M FUNDAMENTALLY INCAPABLE.
AND NOW I'M TWELVE HUNDRED MILES FROM ANYONE WHO CARES.
MURDER
FUCK THIS
IMPERIALIST

PHINEAS RAGE
OLD SCHOOL MOSCOWBILLY -KLEZCORE-
WEDNESDAYS -at- PRISON PLANET
I MEAN, THIS COULD HAVE BEEN THE WORST IDEA I EVER HAD.
EVER.
I AM TALKING ABOUT AN EPIC LEVEL OF FAILURE.
AND I'VE BEEN CONVINCED FOR TWO MONTHS THAT THE FIRST BUMP IN THE ROAD WOULD UNDO ME COMPLETELY.

OKAY, YEAH.
YEAH, I GET IT!
YOU JUST HAD YOUR BUMP.
EXACTLY.
AND YOU'RE FINE!
I AM NOT JUST FINE.
I AM BETTER ENTIRELY.
HA!

I HAVE JUST HAD CONFIRMATION OF MY ADEQUACY AS AN INDEPENDENT ADULT HUMAN.
I PASSED A TEST. I WANT A PRIZE.
I wanna cookie an' a star sticker.
HEH.
YOU'RE AN ADULT?

NO, NO, I'M ASKING FOR REAL.
AH, I'M ONLY KIDDIN.'
YOU'RE LIKE SEVENTEEN, RIGHT?
RAY SAID YOU WERE TWENTY-ONE, BUT SHE LIKES TO MAKE STUFF UP.
SHE KNOWS IT BOTHERS ME.
oh.
UHM, NO. I'M TWENTY-ONE.
TWENTY-ONE FOR REAL.
OH, OKAY!
OKAY.
WOW.
SO.
YOU ARE DEFINITELY, ABSOLUTELY, TOTALLY DONE GROWING, HUH?

WHAT ARE YOU, FIVE-SIX?
. . . YEAH.
LET'S CALL IT FIVE-FIVE.
THAT IS SO COOL.
YOU'RE LIKE A MOVIE STAR.
I DON'T REALLY THINK SO.
NO, IT'S TRUE!
I NEVER GET THE V.I.P. CLIENTS AT WORK, BUT I SEE THOSE GUYS SOMETIMES.
THEY'RE ALL LIKE YOU!
ehn.
WE ARE TRYING TO HAVE A CIVILIZATION HERE
REPORT CRIME • VACCINATE
ATTEND SCHOOL + WORK
WASH + CLEAN
OBEY LAWS
SOCIAL HYGIENE COALITION
TOO BAD YOU'RE NOT YOUNG, THOUGH.
YOUNG-GER, I MEAN.
IT'S FINE AND ALL, BUT I WAS KINDA HOPIN' YOU COULD GET ALONG BETTER WITH EPIPHANY THAT WAY.
EPIPHANY?
PIPPI! MY ROOMMATE, SORT OF.
I THINK YOU'VE SEEN HER.
i think i have.
SHE SAYS SHE HATES YOU, BUT THAT'S JUST A THING SHE DOES.
SHE'S STILL FIGURING OUT WHAT NORMAL PEOPLE ARE LIKE.
DID YOU SMILE AT HER OR SOMETHING? CUZ SHE THINKS THAT'S A TRAP.

WARNING:
THIS COMMUNITY PARTICIPATES IN SKINNER BLOCK WATCH
ALL SUSPICIOUS ACTIVITY IS REPORTED
THIS STREET'S SPONSOR
THE BLACK MARIAH GENTLEWOMAN'S CLUB
I DIDN'T HAVE TIME.
WELL, NO BIG DEAL. SHE DOESN'T LIKE ANY OF MY FRIENDS, YET.
really.
SHE'S AT THAT AGE. WITH THE BEING SO MEAN AND TESTING LIMITS AND STUFF.
I'VE READ SOME BOOKS ABOUT IT. IT'S NORMAL.
I GUESS I UNDERSTAND THAT.
MAD MONK ALE
SHE NEEDS POSITIVE REINFORCEMENT AND GOOD ROLE MODELS.
THAT'S WHAT SHE'LL RESPOND TO.
Cigs + Liqour
CHEMICAL WELFA
BUT SHE DOESN'T HAVE TO IF SHE DOESN'T WANT TO.
I WOULDN'T BLAME HER, IS WHAT I'M SAYING.
EVERYONE WHO'S NICE TO HER JUST ENDS UP IN JAIL.
SCREAMIN' EAGLE
..WHAT?
IT'S VERY COMPLICATED.
LOOK, WE'RE HERE.

24-7-365
KINGDOM COME
GUNS + BOOZE
DEATH + PORN
VICE
XXX
SURPRISED?
NOT EVEN VAGUELY.

OH THANK YOU JEEZUS CHRIST AN' GOD.
WE ARE GOING.
BA-DAM.
GOOD MORNING!
TSSTHT.
NO TALKIN'.
WALK. TURN AN' GO. GORDON.
HIM AGAIN?
REAGAN, THAT MAN NEEDS A SERIOUS PSYCHOLOGICAL INTERVENTION.
NOT MY FUCKIN' DEPARTMENT.
MARCH.
uhm.
uhm, miz mancuso?
ma'am?
SHIT.

WHAT, FLANNERY?
I'M OFF TH' CLOCK, HERE!
uhm, that guy at the back counter, he says— he's on the list, and he wants—
SO TELL 'IM T'PISS OFF! GIVE 'IM TH' LINE!

uhm, he—
he says he has special dispensation? an' he wants to see a manager?
but mister randall isn't in yet?

an' cora's on lunch an' mesmer's hiding in the break room an' no one wants to help me—
OKAY.
and it's just really not a
OKAY, OH-KAY.

oh thank you.
GIMME. AN' I'MA DO THIS ONCE F'YOU, Y'GOT THAT?
YOU GET ONE. SO WATCH.

C'MON, BOYS.
FREAKSHOW'S STARTIN.'

CLAC.

MASTER NO-SELL LIST
HI, GORDON.
FLAP.

GORDON.
HI. WHAT'S UP.
YOU WANNA GUN, GORDON?
NO.

YEAH YOU DO.
NO.
WHERE'S THE OTHER ONE? I WANT HER AGAIN.
BUSY.
AN' FLANNERY SEZ YOU WANT GUNS. I BELIEVE 'ER, TOO, CUZ YOU SNEAK IN HERE EVERY COUPLE MONTHS AN' TRY T'BUY 'EM.
Y'SEE THIS THING I GOT, GORDO?
TELLS ME WHO I CAN'T SELL TO.
THE GUNSMITHS ARE OUT
MASTER - JOURNEYMAN
ASK ABOUT CUSTOM ETCHING
BUT Y'KNOW THAT, CUZ I THROW IT AT YA EVERY TIME YOU WALK THROUGH TH' FUCKIN' DOOR.
AN' YER ON HERE FOUR TIMES, Y'KNOW.
NOW, I GOT A LOTTA GUYS ON TH' NO WEAPONS LIST.
AND I GOT GUYS WITH BOTTLE PROBLEMS. NO BOOZE.
NO MONDO'S SHORTER, CUZ MOST PEOPLE C'N TAKE A LIL' BLOOD.
DISCOUNT FILTH
BUT NO FUCKIN' PORNO NEITHER?
MASTER NO-SELL LIST
THAT'S SOME SPECIAL BOY SHIT RIGHT THERE, GORD.

NOW THIS IS A GODDAM LOVE LETTER FROM YER PAROLE GUY IF I EVER SAW ONE.
AND I'LL BET MY VERY OWN FAT ASS THAT'S CUZ HE KNOWS SUMTHIN' I DON'T.
SO YOU GET NUTHIN' IN HERE. NEVER.
CRINKL.

BUT Y'KNOW, Y'KEEP COMIN' BACK.
SO HERE'S WHUT I FIGGER.
GOD TORTURES CHILDREN
HANS CHRISTIAN ANDERSEN
GRAVE WAXING PHILOSOPHICAL
I FIGGER EITHER YER HOPIN' SOMEONE FORGETS POLICY AN' SELLS T'YOU.
OR YOU JUST LIKE WEIRDIN' OUT TH' COUNTER GIRLS.

CUZ YOU ALWAYS GO FOR TH' GIRLS GORDON, AM I RIGHT?
STANDIN' ALL CLOSE AN' BREATHIN' ALL WET N' SHIT.
GUESS THAT REALLY WORKS GOOD, TOO.
YOU DO TH' SAME DOWN AT SASSY CAVY?
MIGHT GET A FREE PIGGY KABOB OUTTA IT.

OOPS.
TOO ROUGH, HUH?
'KAY, THEN.
BYE.

YOU KNOW TH' DRILL, GORDON.
TWENTY-FOUR HOUR STORE BAN.
wow. you didn't yell at him at all.
NAH, I DON'T DO THAT NO MORE.
THINK IT GETS HIM OFF.

GOOD LORD.
Y'SEE TH' SULKIN'? THAT'S NEW.
IF HE AIN'T GOT SOME POOR GO-TA-PIECES BROAD HE CAN CRAWL INTA WITH THAT GIRL-HATER RAPE-EYE, HE AIN'T GOT NUTHIN.'

FUCKIN' LOON.
NEW STATUES EVERY TEN SECONDS ON KING STREET, BUT CAN'T NOBODY BUILD A CEMENT SIX-BY-SIX FOR THIS GUY.
I JUST HOPE HE'S MEDICATED.
HE DON'T NEED NO FUCKIN' PILL.

I DON'T KNOW. I THINK IT'S SAD.
DON'T YOU THINK IT'S SAD?
BULLSHIT. AIN'T NUTHIN' WRONG WITH THAT GOON AN' OL' FASHIONED BRICK-AN'-BIKE-CHAIN ASS-KICKIN' COULDN'T CLEAN OUT.
SEE HOW CRAZY HE IS WHEN CRAZY'S GOT CONSEQUENCES.

HI.
UHM, WE HAVE THAT WHOLE BOXED COLLECTOR'S EDITION ON CLEARANCE.
IF YOU WANT.
I-
I'M SORRY, WHAT?
THAT FILM.

RETARDED SUCCUBUS
OH.
NO THANKS, I'M JUST... Y'KNOW.
NO.

OH NO, NO. DON'T BE EMBARRASSED.
THIS IS KINGDOM COME.
NOBODY IS GOING TO JUDGE YOU.
TH' FUCK WE AIN'T.
WHA'CHOO GOT THERE, PERV-ASS?

I'M NOT SURE I KNOW.
HA.
HEY, Y'WANT IT? TAKE IT.
WE CAN'T GET RIDDA TH' THING.
I REALLY WOULDN'T KNOW WHAT T'DO WITH IT.

HEALTHY BOY LIKE YOU? YOU'D WORK IT OUT.
HUH.
NOT SURE THAT'S YER COLOR, SUGAR.

IT'S RIOT PAINT.
HE WAS ASSAULTED.
JEEZUS CHRIST, ARE YOU FER REAL?!
WHAT?
OKAY, NO. NO, IT WAS REALLY NOT LIKE THAT.
ASSAULTED?
IT WAS A HOME INVASION BY A WANTED FUGITIVE!
GOD DAMN, WHAT HAPPENED?! DIDJA POP 'IM ONE?
CUZ SEE, I KNOW 'BOUT YOU LITTLE GUYS. YA GOT SUMTHIN' T' PROVE.
I RESPECT THAT SHIT.
TCH!
SOMEONE BROKE INTO YOUR HOUSE AND PAINTED YOU?
THEY'VE MARKED HIS APARTMENT. THEY'RE COMING BACK FOR HIM.
IT WAS ONE GUY!
HE NEEDED MY SINK!
SHOULD SOMEONE CALL THE POLICE?
WOMAN, INVENTORY TH' FUCKIN' BUTT TOYS.

HE HAD A WIG ON. AND A FAKE BEARD.
IT WAS A LITTLE WEIRD, BUT-
A BEARD.
YEAH.
AN' A WIG. AN' RIOT PAINT.

holy *shit.*
HOLY FUCKIN' SHIT, COOKS.
COOK FAMILY.
GAH!!
HOLY SHIT, CAN I TOUCH YOU?!

OH, RAY. REALLY.
WHO SAW TH' NEWS?!
WHO WATCHES TH' GODDAM NEWS, WHAT HAPPENED THIS MORNING?!
SCIP, I *KNOW* YOU WATCH TH' GODDAM NEWS!
WELL, YEAH...

...BUT I'M ON NARROWBAND.
GOOD NEWS ONLY FEED.
GOD DAMN IT SCIP I NEVER FUCKIN' LIKED YOU!

I DON'T LIKE RUINING THE DAY ANY SOONER THAN ABSOLUTELY NECESSARY.
DON'T YOU HAVE A SCREEN IN THE BREAK ROOM OR SOMETHING?
ff+.
ITSA DUMMY BOX.
cook?
GOTTA BE TWENNY YEARS OLD. NUTHIN' ON DEMAND.
PLAYS SHIT WHEN IT'S GOOD AN' READY.

WHAT WAS HE LIKE?
WHAD HE SAY?
ALMOST NOTHING!
STUFF ABOUT COPS. STUFF ABOUT PAINT.
HE DIDN'T STAY LONG.

BUT HE WAS STRAIGHT FUCKIN' SEX, AM I RIGHT?
GOOD-LOOKIN'?
YOU C'N SAY, DON'T MAKE Y'QUEER T' NOTICE.
HE WAS... OLD.
OLD LIKE FIFTY.
RUGGED, HUH?
MM.
MMN.

YOU REALLY KNOW ABOUT THIS GUY? HIS LAST NAME'S COOK?
OH, THEY'RE ALL COOKS, HONEY.
I CAN'T BELIEVE YOU TAKE THAT STUPID DODGE SO SERIOUSLY.

RUINING IT.
DO NOT LISTEN TO HER. IT'S ALL MADE UP. IT'S A FANTASY FOR PARANOIDS AND MALCONTENTS.

SHE GENUINELY BELIEVES THERE'S A SECRET GANG OF ANARCHISTS OUT THERE THAT GETS OFF ON INCITING RIOTS.
I MEAN, SHE THINKS THAT'S A FACT. THAT'S REAL FOR HER.
THEY'RE NOT ANARCHISTS.
'MEMBER THAT ANARCHY MARCH FIVE SUMMERS BACK? THEY BURNED THAT FUCKER DOWN.

THEY DID NOT!
THEY COULDN'T, THEY DON'T EXIST!
BULLSHIT. ANY STUPE IN THIS TOWN WAVES A SIGN AN' IT'S MOLOTOVS ALL OVER.
YOU SAYIN' THAT JUST HAPPENS.
EVERY GODDAM TIME.
NUH-UH. CAN'T ALL BE BANANA OIL. SUMTHIN'S THERE.

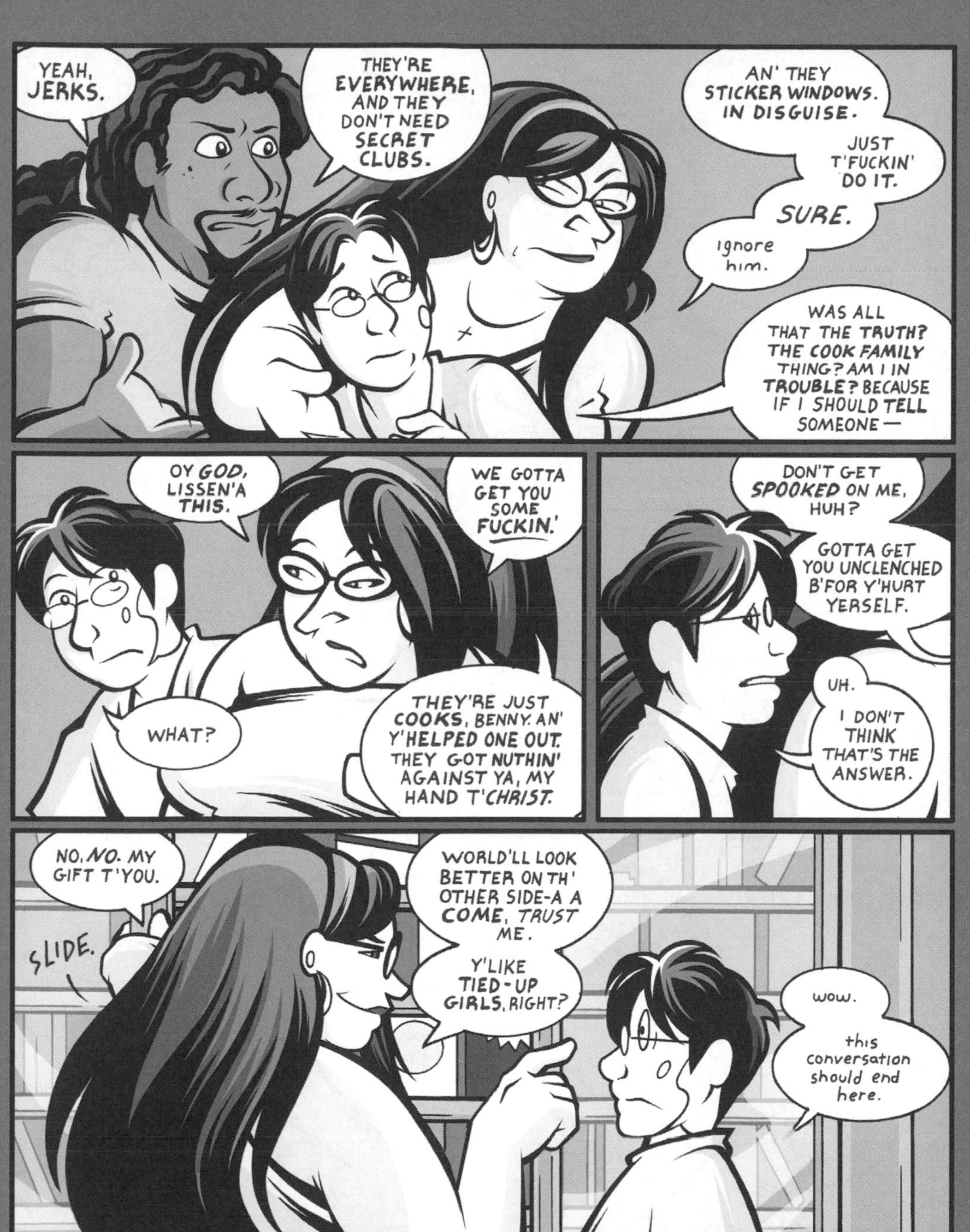
YEAH, JERKS.
THEY'RE EVERYWHERE, AND THEY DON'T NEED SECRET CLUBS.
AN' THEY STICKER WINDOWS. IN DISGUISE.
JUST T'FUCKIN' DO IT.
SURE.
ignore him.
WAS ALL THAT THE TRUTH? THE COOK FAMILY THING? AM I IN TROUBLE? BECAUSE IF I SHOULD TELL SOMEONE —
OY GOD, LISSEN'A THIS.
WE GOTTA GET YOU SOME FUCKIN.'
WHAT?
THEY'RE JUST COOKS, BENNY. AN' Y'HELPED ONE OUT. THEY GOT NUTHIN' AGAINST YA, MY HAND T'CHRIST.
DON'T GET SPOOKED ON ME, HUH?
GOTTA GET YOU UNCLENCHED B'FOR Y'HURT YERSELF.
UH.
I DON'T THINK THAT'S THE ANSWER.
NO, NO. MY GIFT T'YOU.
SLIDE.
WORLD'LL LOOK BETTER ON TH' OTHER SIDE-A A COME, TRUST ME.
Y'LIKE TIED-UP GIRLS, RIGHT?
wow.
this conversation should end here.

YEAH.
YEAH, YOU DIG IT.
YOU DIG IT.
RAY...
I BEEN DOIN' THIS TOO LONG.
I CAN SEE IT IN YA.

TIED-UP GIRLS.
BUT THEY GOTTA BE INTO IT.
RAY.
SEE? SCIP LIKES IT, TOO.

REAGAN!
YOU ARE SO COMPLETELY REPELLENT
IT'S LIKE YOU WERE GROWN FOR IT IN A LAB
GANG-BANGS?
LESBOS?
STUMP-HUMPIN'?
FUNERAL PLAY?
CHICKS SITTIN' ON BIRTHDAY CAKES?
JUST LYING THERE
#7
AMPUTEE
C'MON BUTCH, MAKE A FACE OR SUMTHIN'.

I DO NOT WATCH PORNOGRAPHY.
I REALLY ABSOLUTELY MEAN THAT.
okay.
HN.
NUNNA THIS SEZ BEN, HUH?

FAIR 'NUFF.
WE C'N SKIP TH' FOREPLAY.

FRESH OFF TH' TRUCK.
NEWER'N NEW, KIDDO.
MARCH'A TECHNOLOGY'S HEADED STRAIGHT UP YER—
YOU CAN SAY NO.
THIS ISN'T NECESSARY. WE DON'T HAVE TO BE HERE.
IF WE JUST LEAVE SHE'LL HAVE TO STOP.
oOOo.
WE PROB'LY AIN'T SPOZED T'HAVE THIS.
THINK IT KILLED SOME BROAD IN PHOENIX.
THAT IS GROSS AND NOT TRUE AND I AM WAITING OUTSIDE
UH.
Y'KNOW, I DON'T THINK-
WE GOT TH' WHOLE INTRUDER LINE, BUT Y'WANT MY PROFESSIONAL OPINION?
THE VLAD. PERIOD.
IT'S LIKE BONING TH' FUTURE.
FIFTEEN-SPEED QUIVER CONTROL.
TEXTURIZED PLEASURE NUBLETS.
MEDICAL GRADE SILICONE.
DISHWASHER SAFE.
SHIT'S SO ADVANCED IT NEEDS A SMOKE WHEN YER DONE.
THIS IS SCIENCE, BENNY.
THIS IS TH' COCK OF SCIENCE.
LET TH' COCK OF SCIENCE FUCK YOU.

OOOH. OH, RIGHT.
I GOTTA CUNT'A SCIENCE INNA BACK.
that was not a mistake.
you have been waiting all day to say that.
that is the sort of person you are.
OKAY, WHAT I'M SAYING IS—
I— YEAH, I MEAN—
OW.
ALRIGHT. THERE ARE PEOPLE OUT THERE THAT CALL THEMSELVES COOKS.
BUT THAT DOESN'T MAKE THEM COOKS.
DROP IT.
THEY SAY THEY'RE COOKS BECAUSE THEY'VE HEARD ABOUT COOKS AND THEY WANT TO BE COOKS.
BUT THEY'RE NOT.
DO YOU UNDERSTAND THAT?
DROP IT.
OW.

IT IS BASICALLY AN IMPOSSIBLE THING.
BECAUSE THAT IS NOT A LEGITIMATE ORGANIZATION.
DROP IT, SCIP.
OW OW OW
REAGAN
YOU SAID YOU WOULD STOP WHEN IT STARTED TO HURT
YEAH, I SAY THAT TO A LOTTA PEOPLE.
I'M MAKING A POINT.
SCIP, WHERE YOU THINK ORG'NIZATIONS COME FROM?
IF THEY SAY THEY'RE COOKS AN' THEY DO PEOPLE LIKE COOKS, THAT MAKES 'EM GODDAM COOKS.
AHOW
HA! BIG PIECE!
THAT'S MOSTLY SKIN
tsk.
THAT IS NOT HOW THINGS WORK.
fft. YEAH. IT IS.
COOKS ARE A SPECIFIC THING, REAGAN, NOT AN IDEA.
YOU DON'T EVEN THINK THEY'RE REAL!
THEY DON'T HAVE TO BE REAL TO HAVE A DEFINITION.
AW JEEZIS CHRIST—
nn.
YOU TWO ARE WORSE THAN MY PARENTS.

HA HA. SHIT.
DAMN.
SORRY.
SORRY.
BUT IT'S– YOU GUYS HEAR YOURSELVES, DON'T YOU?
YOU SOUND LIKE YOU'VE BEEN SLEEPING IN THE SAME BED FOR THIRTY YEARS.
I DON'T THINK YOU CAN BE NORMAL AROUND EACH OTHER.
IS THAT WRONG?
BECAUSE I HAVEN'T SEEN IT.

...I'M NORMAL. I AM ABSOLUTELY VERY NORMAL.
YOU CAN'T REALLY BELIEVE THAT I'M NOT.
ha.
I KNOW. I KNOW YOU ARE.
BECAUSE I NOTICE THE DIFFERENCE.
YOU OPERATE ON A COMPLETELY SEPARATE LEVEL OF INTENSITY WHEN REAGAN'S THERE.
SCIPIO SQUARED.
HA!

YOU TOO.
ME TOO, HUH.
YOU GAVE ME A SPEECH ABOUT DILDOS.
THAT'S TH' JOB.
YOU TOOK IT OUT OF THE BOX AND YOU HIT ME WITH IT.
REAGAN IS AN AFFRONT TO CIVIL DECENCY.
SHE LIVES TO HEAR YOU SAY THAT.
DECENCY.
THIS FROM TH' GUY WHAT SHAVES HIS PUBES INTA LIL' SHAPES.
I DO NOT!
BUNNIES N'SHIT. BUTTERFLIES.
KIDS ON BIKES.
HOW WOULD YOU EVEN KNOW THAT
you're doing it.
AAAM-BER TOLD ME.
JESUS CHRIST YOU ARE JUST MENTALLY INCAPABLE OF RETIRING THE SUBJECT.
I AIN'T NEVER GONNA LET YOU FORGET DRAGGIN' THAT ONE IN TH' DOOR.
GODDAM FLOOR MODEL DOWN AT TH' DUMMY STORE.
AAAM-BER.
YEAH, AND LUCKY WAS A ROCKET SURGEON.

OH FUCK YOU, OKAY? LUCKY WAS ALL RIGHT.
LUCKY.
IT IS NOT EVEN A PERSON NAME. IT IS A DOG NAME.
HOW COULD THAT BE INTERPRETED AS ANYTHING BUT A TERRIBLE WARNING?
LUCKY.
MN.
PICK
PICK
PICK
CURIO.
I HAVE NEVER DATED CURIO.
AW WOOOW, I KNOW EXACTLY HOW YOU LOOOW PEOPLE FEEEL. I'VE SEEN A MIIILION DOCUMENTARIES.
TEE FUCKIN' HEE.
PYEW.
THAT IS EXTREMELY UNFAIR AND SHE NEVER SAID THAT AND SHE DOES NOT SOUND THAT WAY.
CUZ YOU GOT YER TONGUE OUTTA HER MOUTH LONG ENUFF FOR A LISTEN.
WE NEVER DATED.
GUYS?
WHAT, IT WAS JUST FUCKIN'?
CLASS.
REAGAN GOD DAMN IT
WHY DO YOU HATE EVERYBODY
GUYS? SHOULD WE BE WAVING BACK?

YUP.
THAT'S THEM.
NO SHIT, MOZE.
THANK YOU.
THANKS.
COULDN'T TELL.
REALLY.
MONSTERS OF DEMOCRACY

BLOCK AN' A HALF AWAY AN' YOU COULD TAKE GODDAMNED **DICTATION**.
EMBARRASSING.
FUCKIN' **DISGRACE** IS WHAT IT IS.
THEY SEE US.
SUPERMANDINGO AN' **TONS OF FUN** BETTER PUT A CHAIN ON TH' **RACE WAR** T'DAY, CUZ I'M **NOT** IN TH' MOOD.
I AM **NOT** HAVIN' THIS. MY DAYS ARE TOO DAMNED LONG, OKAY?
I AIN'T WALKIN' DOWN TH' STREET WITH THAT.

YOU SOUND TIRED.
WE COULD JUST GO HOME.
I GOT A MOTHER, **YETI.**
WHO'S THE **LITTLE ONE?**

I DUNNO. NEW. RAY SAID THEY WERE GONNA BE PLUS ONE.
FOR *THIS?*
HE'S DOWN? **HIM?** HE DON'T *LOOK* DOWN.
EH.
i'm being pointed at.

FLICK
FLICK
FLICK
game's over.

over.
mmh. i need a fire.

AW HELL.
SUNNY.
FUCKIN' SHUT IT.
GENE.
GENE, Y'GOTTA DO BETTER.
D'WE NEED TO RUN? IS IT COPS?

no.
NO COPS. GUYS IN UNIFORMS. CUFFS AN' GUNS.
i know how cops do.

it's not cops. it's eric.

i'm sorry.

ERIC? **RED ERIC?!**

ERIC WITH TH' *DENT?*

THIRD TIME THIS SEASON.

HOW'S HE EVEN KNOW WHEN A MATCH IS ON?

A GODDAMN RAT!

SOME MISERABLE LAST-PLACE **SHIT** SNITCHIN' ON THE **LIVE FIELDS!**

ERIC PUNCHES ENOUGH HOLES IN TH' LINE-UP, TH' **WHOLE SEASON'S** *SHOT!*

I **HATE** THIS FUCKIN' GAME AN' EVERY **SNIVELIN' BITCH** PLAYIN' IT!

WHAT GAME?

...ben.

eric is playin' **diesel**, ben.

BEN, RIGHT.

"DIESEL."

LIKE GAS, HUH?

nooo, like *hockey*.

OH.

yeah.

but it's over t'day.

cuz it can't start.

SO THAT'S HIM IN THE MIDDLE.
YES. DEFINITELY, ABSOLUTELY.
I'VE SEEN A PHOTOGRAPH.
THAT IS RED ERIC.
REAGAN, WHY WOULD I *LIE?*
HIS INITIALS ARE RIGHT THERE ON HIS **SAMSON**.

WHAT. C'MON.
THAT IS TH' ALPHA FUCKIN' MALE? TH' LEGEND?
GOTTA FACE LIKE A DAMN BABOON.
MONKEY WITH A DIRT-STACHE.
REAGAN, WE DO NOT LIVE IN THE MOVIES.
BRAIN-DAMAGED SOCIOPATHS TEND TO LOOK LIKE BRAIN-DAMAGED SOCIOPATHS.
I DON'T EVEN GET RED HAIR.
CAN'T EVEN SWING THAT.
"RED ERIC" MY ASS.
NO, NO. HE JUST LIKES STALIN A WHOLE LOT. AND BLEEDING.
THEY ALL JUST GONNA STAND THERE?
MAYBE. THEY'RE JUMPING THE MATCH.
IF THE OTHER TEAMS CAN'T GET THEM OFF THE FIELD, RED ERIC AND THE GET-UPS WIN THE SPOT THEY WERE PLAYING FOR.
OR THEY WOULD, IF THEY WERE STILL IN THE LEAGUE.
THEY WERE VOTED OUT A YEAR AGO. I DON'T KNOW WHY THEY BOTHER.
HE DOESN'T WANT TH' SPOT, TINY. HE'S HERE T' BREAK HEADS.
IT'S ALL HE'S FUCKIN' GOOD FOR!

YOU HEAR ME, YOU LIVING SHIT?!
WE GOT YOUR FUCKIN' NUMBER!
IF THIS THING HERE WEREN'T ILLEGAL WE'D HAVE EVERY PIG IN TOWN ON YER ASS!

SAL. DUMAS. SALAMANDER.
MVP CENTER FOR TH' LOWBALLERS. LEGEND IN PROGRESS.
ASK ME WHAT THAT WASTE DID T'SAL.
ASK ME HOW MANY TEETH SAL'S GOT LEFT.

TELL YOU WHAT NEEDS T'GO DOWN, ME AN' MOZE AN' TH' DARK CONTINENT OVER THERE?
WE NEED T'GET ERIC ON HIS OWN AN' SELL WHAT'S LEFT BY TH' POUND.

S'WHAT I'M FUCKIN' THINKIN'.

SUNNY USE'TA PLAY.
ERIC BROKE HIS ANKLES.
ANKLE, SINGULAR.
BREAK AN' A SPRAIN.
YOU FAT SLANDERING FUCK.

AND YER ASS OUGHTA BE DOWN THERE LICKIN' HIS BALLS FOR IT!
IF I'DA NEVER BEEN CRIPPED, YOU'D STILL BE DOIN' THREE-HOUR SHRED GUITAR SETS FOR BEER IN THAT SHIT FALKYN COVER BAND!
ha ha.
YEAH, GET HAPPY, ÜBERMENSCH.
I FOUND YER ASS PLAYIN' TH' SIDEWALK WITH A DAMN TIP JAR.
YER NO FUCKIN' DIFFERENT.
MUSICIANS ARE ALL RETARDS.
YOU DRUM.
A MONKEY COULD DO WHAT I DO!
OUTTA TEN, I'MA SIX. SEVEN, MAYBE.
YOU DUMB SACKS'A SHIT ARE ELEVENS.
DON'T COMPARE, IT IS DELUSIONAL.
ARE YOU GUYS IN GENE'S BAND?
BORNDOWN.
YES.
ME.
HIM.
THAT.
AN' BO, WHO AIN'T HERE.
SKIPPED PRACTICE T'GO GET AIDS.
i'm not retarded.

HEH. YEAH, WELL, Y'BANNED GIRLFRIENDS FROM REHERSAL.
THAT'S GONNA HAPPEN.
BULL SHIT, IT IS NOT.
I GOT A BUSINESS T'RUN, THIS IS WORK WE ARE DOIN'!
I can read.
YOU DON'T SHOW UP FOR WORK, YOU GET FIRED.
THERE'S NO EXCUSE. ANY ONE'A YOU JACKOFFS NEEDS A LAY, Y'GOT TH' OARLOCK RIGHT THERE.
IT'S IN TH' BUDGET. YOU'VE SEEN TH' DAMN SPREADSHEET.
CUZ I HAVE FILLED MY CRAZY BITCH WIFE CHASIN'-OFF QUOTA FOR THIS BAND, THAT I WILL SWEAR T'GOD.
AN' I WILL NOT BE FUCKIN' TESTED ON THIS.
DOGSBODY COURIERS
EMMA WASN'T SO BAD.
SHE COULD BAKE.
...
EMMA MARRIED GENE, MOZE.
GENE.
THAT'S NOT FUNNY.

EH! HE'S JAKESKIN. YOU KNOW HOW THEY GET.
PROB'LY GOT TEN MORE RUNNIN' AROUND.
AN' THEY BETTER STAY OFF TH' FUCKIN' MAP, TOO!
NEXT JAKE CUNT WAVIN'A MACHETE AT ME DON'T GET TA KEEP HER TEETH.

I DIDN'T KNOW YOU WERE MARRIED.
ben. hey.
i married emma.

we made zora.
and that's why.
you got stuff on you here.
look at it.

OH, YEAH.
IT WON'T, UH.
DOESN'T WANNA COME OFF.
did you fall?
I DID, ACTUALLY.
ow.
IT'S FINE, I'M FINE.

IZZAT WHAT SMELLS LIKE A DUMPTRUCK?
AW NO, STILL?
LIKE RIGHT NOW?
IS IT BUGGING YOU?

EH.
SORRY. I'M *REALLY* SORRY, YOU SHOULD HAVE SAID SOMETHING.
SORRY.
NAH, I DUNNO HOW TA TELL A GUY SUMTHIN' LIKE THAT.
YOU JUST ***DID.***
BEN, RIGHT? YEAH, I'M RIGHT.
BEN, YOU NEED **DEGREASER.**
RIOT PAINT, AIN'T IT?
DEGREASER. ***SOLVENT.***
SUMTHIN' WITH A **SWEET SMELL.**
SMELLS SWEET, IT'LL WORK, GETCHA STRAIGHT.
CRINKLE.
REALLY?
DUMP IT ON A RAG AN' RUB IT IN.
DON'T **LEAVE IT** THOUGH, WASH AFTER.
FUCKS UP YOUR SPERM.
OR NERVES.
CRUNCH
SMACK.
DON'T REMEMBER.
SHIT, THEY GOT Y'GOOD. BET THAT ***STUNG.***

THAT'S NOT HOW I—
YEAH, I'M DOWN.
Y'WOKE UP WITH IT.
MAGIC. SURE.
RELAX. YER IN TH' SHADE WITH ME, Y'FUCKER.
YOU THINK I DUNNO?
I KNOW.
SO WHAT WENT RUNNIN,' HAH?
COP FIGHT?
GOOD ONE?
USE'TA WEAR MY PAINT AROUND, TOO.
WAR WOUNDS.
SHIT YEAH.
uh.
BET THEY NEVER SUSPECT A DAMN THING, NEITHER.
TH' GLASSES? TOO GODDAM PERFECT.
BET T.P. NEVER LOOKS TWICE B'FORE TH' HAMMER DROPS.
HA.
STILL GOT SKUNKED.
A SMOKE'LL KILL TH' STINK.
I'M GOOD.
SO WHAT'M I MISSIN', THOSE TWO GOIN' STEADY NOW?
LIL' GUY REMINDS SUNNY OF HISSELF.
TH' FUCK?
OH MY GAWD.

THUTMOSE!
RA!
EUGENE, HI!
KKhk.
OH MY GOD. WHY DIDN'T THEY CALL ME?!
EVERYBODY'S HERE! I DIDN'T KNOW THERE WAS GONNA BE A THING!
C'MON, LET'S GO!
WHO ARE THEY?
FRIENDS, BITCH.
GET SOME.
DO THEY KNOW THAT?
FUCK YOU, TUESDAY.
ben. I seen that girl naked.
ME TOO!
Me Too.
MOZE, DO NOT.
NAH. I'M GONNA.
WE GOTTA START CHARGIN' HER ADMISSION.
BE NICE.

WHY? YOU STILL TRYIN' T'GET SOME?
JESUS CHRIST REAGAN PLEASE STOP.
OH MY GOD THIS IS SO LUCKY!
I HAVEN'T SEEN YOU GUYS IN FOREVER!
SHOVE.
OKAY, TUESDAY? D'YOU REMEMBER THAT INCREDIBLE AUTHENTIC TOTALLY ILLEGAL CLUB I TOLD YOU ABOUT?
THE ONE IN THE RIVERBED WITH THE FIGHTS?
THESE GUYS WERE PLAYING THERE.
RIGHT.
IT WAS SO COMPLETELY FERAL.
THAT WAS BACK BEFORE EVERYBODY WAS INTO BORNDOWN, Y'KNOW?
I GOT BACKSTAGE. WE HUNG OUT BASICALLY FOREVER.
SHOP TALK.
MM.
THINK I SAW A REVIEW FOR YOUR LAST ALBUM IN TEMPLAR DAMAGE REPORT.
YEAH? HOW'D WE DO?

NINE POINT TWO IS HOW WE DID.
OH HEY, THAT'S GOOD.
NO, THAT IS SHIT. THAT IS NOTHING.
IT IS WHITE GODDAMNED NOISE.
DAMAGE REPORT? FUCKIN' PLEASE.
AND FUCK NICKY. SHIT ON NICKY.
NICKY? NICKY COLLISION?
YES.
HE'S BEEN DOIN' REVIEWS FREELANCE EVER SINCE SAVAGE RECORDS ATE HIS BULLSHIT WANNA-BE PROG ROCK JERK CIRCLE ALIVE.
CAN'T GET HIRED T'PLAY A COFFEE SHOP. SO NOW HE'S SOME GLITTER-SHITTIN' QUEER-FOR-THE-CAMERAS SCENE CREATURE SUCKIN' EVERY DICK HE STOMPED ON HIS WAY TO TH' TOP.
BITCH NEVER EVEN MADE IT TO TH' MIDDLE.
HEE HEE.
YEAH, IT'S EVEN FUNNIER IF YER ME.
NICKY GAVE MY SHOW A TWO POINT SIX.
UH-HUH, SO YOU'LL MENTION HIS FAME-GRUBBIN' ASS ON AIR.
HE CAN SHIT ON YOU ALL HE WANTS, YOU'RE NOT INDUSTRY.

WHAT IF YOU GUYS GET SIGNED?
Y'KNOW, TO A MAJOR LABEL.
WILL HE CALL YOU SELL-OUTS? BECAUSE THE HYPOCRISY WOULD BE TOXIC.
I'LL NEVER KNOW, CUZ I'M SMARTER'N NICKY AN' I KNOW BETTER'N T'PIMP MY EXISTENCE TO TH' HIGHEST BIDDER.
ANYONE IN BORNDOWN WANTS T'BE ON TH' COVER OF SUGAR OR GRAPEVINE, THEY'RE IN TH' WRONG FUCKIN' BAND.
THEY KNOW THAT GOING IN?
I RUN A TRANSPARENT GOD DAMNED OPERATION.
HEY TUESDAY, THUTMOSE IS NILE.
YOU SHOULD PUT HIM ON YOUR SHOW!
RA, TOO! THEY'RE COUSINS.
MM.
"SUNNY."
HE DON'T DIG "RA."
AW, REALLY? NILE NAMES ARE SO PRETTY, THOUGH.
CALLIN' HIM "RA" JUST MAKES 'IM WANNA SOCK YOU.
oh!
OH, UHM.
M'SORRY.
BO TOLD ME—
WELL I GUESS BO THINKS YOU NEED A SOCK, CURIO.

HEY.
I LIKE YER NAKED DANCIN'.
FREEFORM NATURALIST EURYTHMY.
NAH, THAT'S LONGER T'SAY.
MORE GIRLS OUGHTA TAKE THEIR CLOTHES OFF WHERE I CAN SEE IT.
MM-HM.
Y'SHOULDN'T **SHAVE YOUR BUSH,** THOUGH. YOU GOT **NO TITS,** SO IT MAKES ME FEEL **WEIRD.**
YOU SHOULD DYE IT LIKE YOUR HAIR. **BLUE BUSH** WOULD BE COOL.
MM-HMM.
OOPS. ARE YOU MAD?
NO.
M' SORRY.
I'M FINE. YOU CAN'T OFFEND ME.
OH, GOOD.
SO D'YOU FUCK **GUYS?** CUZ YOU KINDA GOT THIS **LEZZIE** VIBE.
AN' I **LOVE YOU,** SO I GOTTA KNOW HOW SAD I SHOULD BE.
WHAT?
IT'S TH' WRONG KINDA LOVE, THOUGH. IT'S **DIRTY LOVE.**
SO Y'DON'T HAFTA LOVE BACK. CUZ I'M ALL FAT N'HAIRY N'SHIT.
RIGHT.
BUT I GOTTA DICK LIKE **A BEER CAN.**
WE COULD TURN OUT TH' LIGHTS. YOU WOULD LIKE IT.
uh.
i sing.
i do guitar.

Y'COULD PRETEND I WAS A GIRL.
I GOT TITS.
an' concertina. an' banjo.
piano. trumpet. saxophone.
uhm.
i dunno, it's from australia.
it's long. you blow in it.
RIGHT.
violin.
mandolin, panpipes, baryton, crumhorn.
ER.
saw.
and, uhm.
okay. that's all.
but most times it's singing.
then guitar.
what do you play?
WELL, Y'MEAN?
NOTHING.
how can it be nothing?
I HAD PIANO LESSONS WHEN I WAS A KID.
BUT IT DIDN'T STICK.
it can't be nothing.
NO, REALLY.
oh, no.
I ONLY WRITE, I GUESS.
TRY TO.

UHM. HI.
'SCUSE ME.
HI.
HI.
UHM- DO YOU-
ARE YOU REALLY A WRITER?
FOR A LIVING?
I WAS LISTENING, AND UH.
YEAH, SO FAR.
OH MY GOD. THAT IS SO INCREDIBLE.
IT'S EASIER THAN IT LOOKS.
do you whistle?
NOT REGULARLY.
OH, NO NO NO, IT'S SO COOL! I WANNA WRITE, TOO!
SERIOUSLY! I HAVE WANTED TO WRITE FOR-EVER.
BUT I DON'T KNOW WHAT TO DO.
AND I ASK PEOPLE AND THEY'RE ALL "Y'JUST DO IT" AND I CAN'T.
I WRITE, BUT I DON'T WRITE, Y'KNOW?

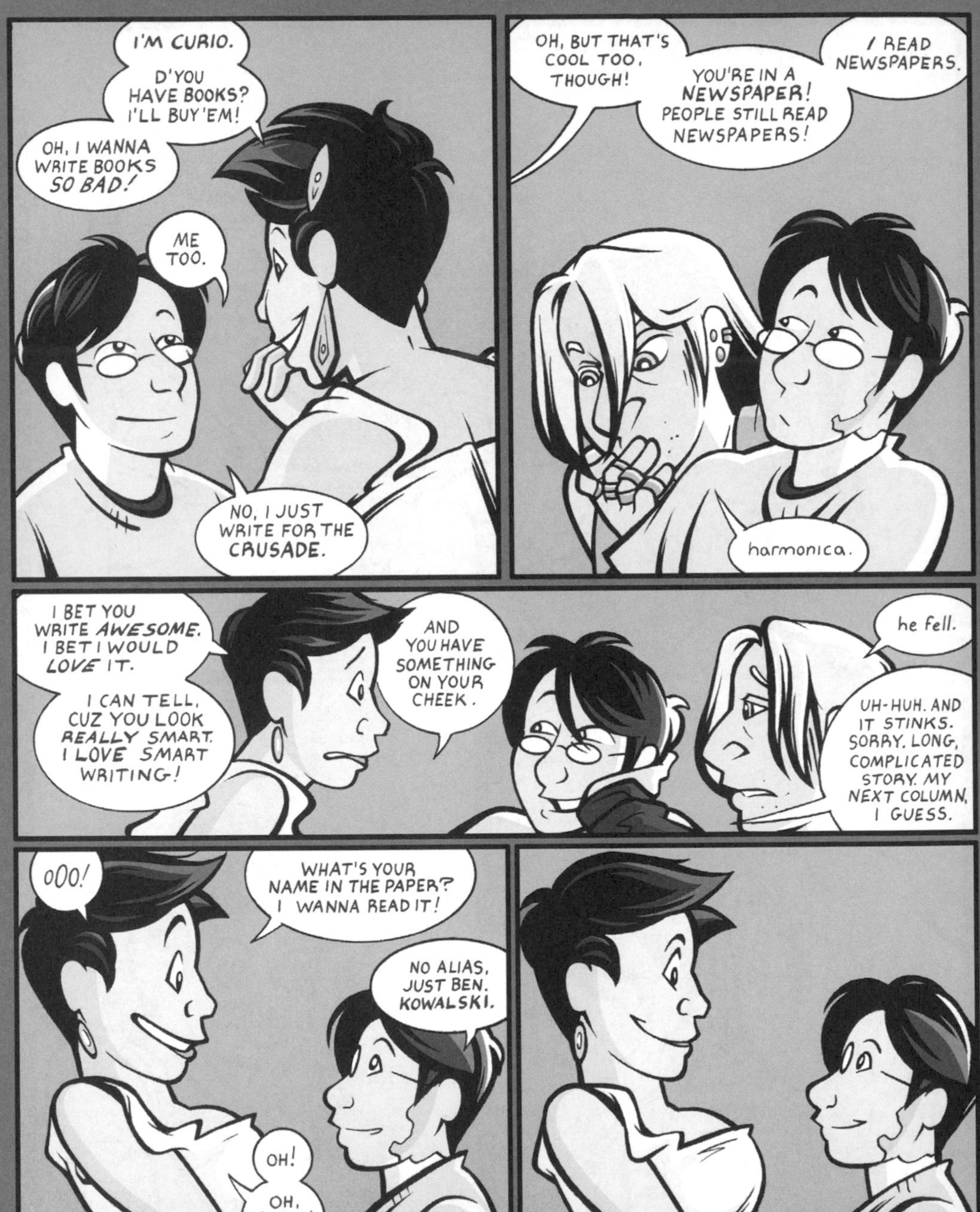

I'M CURIO.
D'YOU HAVE BOOKS? I'LL BUY 'EM!
OH, I WANNA WRITE BOOKS SO BAD!
ME TOO.
NO, I JUST WRITE FOR THE CRUSADE.
OH, BUT THAT'S COOL TOO, THOUGH!
YOU'RE IN A NEWSPAPER! PEOPLE STILL READ NEWSPAPERS!
I READ NEWSPAPERS.
harmonica.
I BET YOU WRITE AWESOME. I BET I WOULD LOVE IT.
I CAN TELL, CUZ YOU LOOK REALLY SMART. I LOVE SMART WRITING!
AND YOU HAVE SOMETHING ON YOUR CHEEK.
he fell.
UH-HUH. AND IT STINKS. SORRY. LONG, COMPLICATED STORY. MY NEXT COLUMN, I GUESS.
oOO!
WHAT'S YOUR NAME IN THE PAPER? I WANNA READ IT!
NO ALIAS, JUST BEN. KOWALSKI.
OH!
OH, OKAY!

CAN I ASK YOU A PERSONAL QUESTI-
ADOPTED. YEAH.
OH MY GAWD, I KNOW, I WAS GONNA SAY!
CUZ I WAS ALL, "NUH-UH, THAT IS A POLISH NAME!"
AND YOU'RE ASIAN.
I WAS GONNA SAY!
BUT THAT'S JUST ME, Y'KNOW?
I WANNA KNOW ABOUT PEOPLE! I ASK A TON OF QUESTIONS.
IT'S LIKE, I WANNA BE RIGHT THERE IN TH' MOMENT.
I THINK I CAN SEE THAT.
IT'S IMPORTANT TO ASK QUESTIONS AND KNOW PEOPLE.
REAL PEOPLE.
THAT'S WHY I LIKE IT DOWN HERE SO MUCH, EVERYBODY'S REAL-ER.
DOWN WHERE?
OH!
UHM, I LIVE UPTOWN. KING STREET.
BUT REALLY, I AM TOTALLY NOT LIKE ANY PERSON THERE.
REALLY. I HATE THEM.
THEY SHOULD DIE.
GENE! C'MON. WE'RE GOING!

YOU'RE GENE, RIGHT?

THAT'S HIM.

YEAH.

SO C'MON, LET'S GET OUTTA HERE.

WAIT, *WHAT?*

SCRATCH.

YOU JUST SAYIN' THAT SO I DON'T THINK YOU'RE A SLUT?
CUZ I DON'T MIND.
TSK. YOU HUNGRY, SUNNY?
I CAN GET US INTO PANGAEA.
PAN-CONTINENTAL FUSION.
CAJUN LLAMA STIR FRY TO DIE FOR.
DEEP FRIED SUGAR
'M GOOD.
AW C'MON, WE'LL TRASH NICKY SOME MORE. I WANNA HEAR ALL YOUR ROCK BAND DRAMA.
NO GOD DAMN IT, I'M GOIN' HOME, I GOT WORK.
WE GOT AN ALBUM GOIN' OUT IN THREE WEEKS.
WHO'S GONNA PUT TOGETHER TH' PRESS KITS?!
HIM?!
NAH.
YOU KNOW I DON'T DO NUTHIN.'
FUCKIN' EXACTLY.
TAKE GOBLIN.
NO!
WELL.
JUST US THREE, THEN.
OR FOUR, MAYBE?
ARE YOU WITH TH' BAND?
ME?
HA. NO.

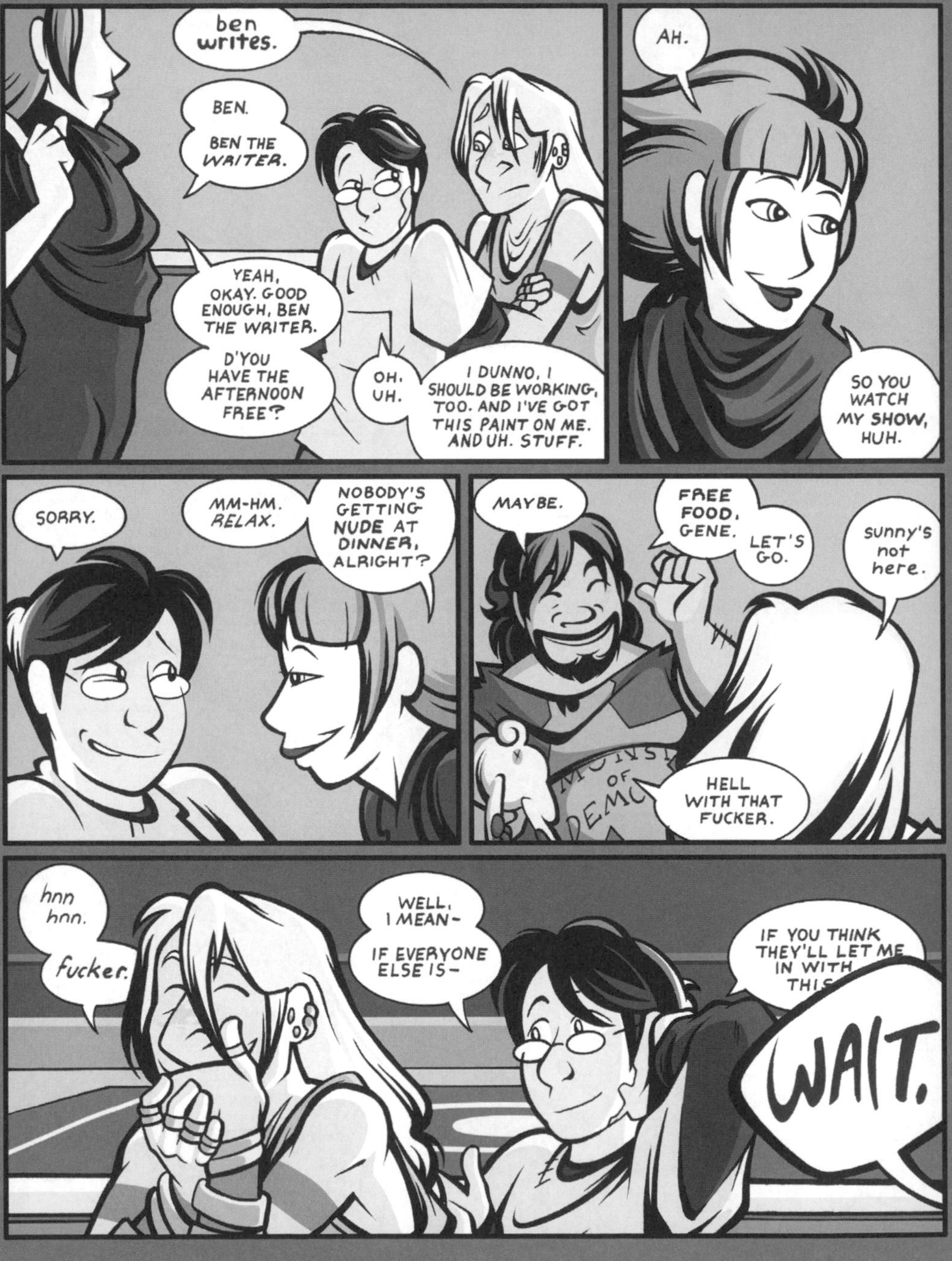

ben writes.
BEN.
BEN THE WRITER.
YEAH, OKAY. GOOD ENOUGH, BEN THE WRITER.
D'YOU HAVE THE AFTERNOON FREE?
OH, UH.
I DUNNO, I SHOULD BE WORKING, TOO. AND I'VE GOT THIS PAINT ON ME. AND UH. STUFF.
AH.
SO YOU WATCH MY SHOW, HUH.
SORRY.
MM-HM. RELAX.
NOBODY'S GETTING NUDE AT DINNER, ALRIGHT?
MAYBE.
FREE FOOD, GENE.
LET'S GO.
sunny's not here.
HELL WITH THAT FUCKER.

hnn hnn.
fucker.
WELL, I MEAN-
IF EVERYONE ELSE IS-
IF YOU THINK THEY'LL LET ME IN WITH THIS
WAIT.

YOU CAN'T!
YOU CAN'T GO.
WE'RE BUSY, GUYS! WE WERE GONNA DO STUFF!
WE WERE?
OH MY GOD YES I WAS GONNA ASK!
I WAS GONNA ASK ABOUT THE MISSION.
THEY'RE HAVING RITES.
WE TOTALLY HAVE TO SEE.
I DON'T KNOW WHAT THAT IS.
OH!
OH. IT'S, UHM!
A PARTY, SORT OF? A FESTIVAL.
THE MISSION IN OLD TOWN HAS A BUNCH EVERY YEAR. ALL THE RELIGIONS THERE DO 'EM TOGETHER!
THERE'S GONNA BE DERVISHES AN' GUYS DANCING WITH SNAKES? THEY'RE GONNA BURY A YOGI!
AN' SOME MONKS ARE GONNA DRAW WITH SAND.
WAIT, YOU MEAN A MANDALA?
REALLY?
THAT'S TODAY?
AIN'T THEM MISSION BUDDHISTS SICK'A YOU YET, SCIP?
ALL LAMAS ARE HAPPY TO PROVIDE BLESSINGS OF MERIT AND MORAL INSTRUCTION.
HOLY SHIT YOU TOTAL FUCKIN' JERKOFF.

I AM NOT A JERKOFF. I JUST FIND THEIR DEVOTION VERY MOVING.
YEAH WELL, I MOVE PLENTY ALREADY.
SO, Y'GOT ROOM FER ONE MORE, BALDY?
I AIN'T WITH **BORNDOWN**, BUT I'M *REAL* POOR.
THAT'S WHAT'CHA CAME FOR, AIN'T IT?
OH, NO. NO *NO* ***NO,*** DO ***NOT*** TAKE HER.
THIS IS A **TRICK**, SHE IS A ***HORROR***.
DRY UP, HUH? I'M TRYIN'A GET **FED** HERE.
REAGAN, YOU WERE NOT *INVITED*.
SHE DOESN'T EVEN *KNOW* YOU.
SHE DON'T KNOW **GENE**. SHE DON'T KNOW **MOZE** AN' **BEN**.
YOU CAN COME.
EVERYONE CAN COME, I *WANT* YOU TO.
OH.
AN' **THERE** YA **FUCKIN'** ***GO***.
WITH **MANNERS** EVEN.

EVERYONE. THAT MEANS ME.
AND YOU.
AND I WOULD GO.
I ABSOLUTELY WOULD.
IF IT WEREN'T FOR RITES.
YOU GUYS ARE COMING TOO, RIGHT?
SURE.
IT SOUNDS INTERESTING.
EH. FUCK IT. GO WATCH YER MONKS.
PANGAEA PROB'LY DON'T GOT NO ORGANIC FREE-RANGE GRASS CLIPPIN' SPECIAL ANYHOW.
I'LL BRING BACK A DOGGIE BAG SO'S YOU C'N STILL BITCH ABOUT WHAT I ORDER.
FUNNY.
SCIP.
SCIP, GENE. BEN THE WRITER.
GONNA REMEMBER YOU THREE.
OKAY. SEE YOU. BYE.
CURIO'S GOT MY NUMBER.
YOU GOTTA LEAVE AFTER WE EAT. CUZ OF TH' FUCKIN'.
YEAH, I'MA TUNE IN NEXT MONDAY T'HEAR HOW SHIT YOU WERE.

TSK.
HOW FAR IS OLD TOWN?
OH! UHM, NOT FAR?
NOT TOO FAR.
WE COULD WALK IT, BUT IT'S KINDA WARM OUT.
WE SHOULD TAKE THE TUNNELS, THEY'RE FREE ON WEEKENDS.
IS IT NEAR KING STREET? I KNOW WHERE THAT IS.

NO.
WHERE D'YOU FIND OUT ABOUT THESE KINDA THINGS?
I DIDN'T EVEN KNOW THIS WAS HAPPENING.
I THINK THERE'S A CHANNEL YOU CAN SUBSCRIBE TO.
are we goin' somewhere?
RITES.
WHEN ARE THEY STARTING THE MANDALA?

DECEMBER.
SCRATCH
SCRATCH

UH, CURIO? IF IT'S NOT UNTIL-
I KNOW, I KNOW
I'M SORRY, I AM SO FUCKIN' SORRY.

YOU DO NOT UNDERSTAND IT, OKAY?
TUESDAY MADE ME BRING HER
CUZ SHE SAID I DON'T KNOW YOU AND I DO!
AND SHE'S A FUCKIN' BITCH AND A FRIEND STEALER AND YOU CAN'T GO WITH HER!
EVERYTHING SHE SAYS IS SO YOU HATE ME!

AND YOU CAN HATE ME NOW IF YOU WANT CUZ I FUCKED UP
BUT NOT CUZ SHE TOLD YOU TO!

WHAM!
LM
AW!
LAVENDER MENACE

"WARNING: CONTACT WITH LIQUID OR MIST FORM OF PRODUCT MAY CAUSE IRRITATION."
"OVEREXPOSURE TO VAPORS CAN RESULT IN DIZZINESS, LOSS OF CONCENTRATION, LUNG AND EYE DAMAGE, AND DEFATTING OF THE SKIN."
OH, WOW.
JEEZ.
THIS STUFF IS REALLY **AWFUL**, BEN.
HOW D'YOU FEEL?
LIKE.
LIKE I'M AT THE BOTTOM.
BOTTOM OF A SWIMMING POOL.

BOTTOM LOOKING UP.
"DEFATTING OF THE SKIN."
DEFATTING OF THE SKIN.
THAT CAN'T BE WHAT I'M THINKING. WHAT I'M THINKING IS COMPLETELY HORRIBLE.
hnn hnn.
WELL, AT LEAST IT WORKS.
BUT IF SUNNY'S BEEN SLOSHING AROUND IN THIS POISON, IT KINDA EXPLAINS WHY HE BEHAVES LIKE A RABID WHOOPS!
ha!
TILT.
NO.
NO NO M'SORRY.
M'FINE.
S-SORRY.
UHM.
OH-KAY.
OKAY, THAT WHOLE FALLING OVER THING YOU JUST DID?
I'M REALLY NOT TOO HAPPY WITH THAT.
IF YOU DO THAT AGAIN, YOU SHOULD MAYBE SEE SOMEONE ABOUT IT.

I'M OKAY, IT'S OVER.
THANK YOU.
IF YOU'RE SURE.
I AM.
hnh!
ben threw off his prophet.
WHAT?
NO, BEN IS SOAKED IN AN INDUSTRIAL SOLVENT ON THE RECOMMENDATION OF A HABITUAL VIOLENT OFFENDER.
you gotta let em ride you.
I'M BETTER.
JUST GLAD THE PAINT'S OFF.
BILL SAID IT WAS GONNA TAKE DAYS.
"BILL" PROBABLY VALUES HIS BRAIN FUNCTION TOO MUCH TO EVEN CONSIDER THIS.
FIVE MINUTES WORKING BORNDOWN'S SECURITY AND I KNEW THERE WAS SOMETHING WRONG WITH SUNNY'S HEAD.
BUT I ALWAYS ASSUMED IT WAS A BLUNT FORCE TRAUMA THING.
NOT A CHEMICAL.

YOU WORKED FOR SUNNY?
SOMETIMES. USED TO.
JUST ONCE, HONESTLY.
I WASN'T GETTING ANY HOURS DOWN AT THE FIRM A WHILE BACK, SO I DID SOME BACKSTAGE STUFF FOR THE BAND.

I REALLY CAN'T DO THAT AGAIN.
I'M NO GOOD AT THAT KINDA THING.
I GUESS IT MIGHTA BEEN OKAY A COUPLE YEARS AGO, BEFORE THEY GOT POPULAR?
BUT EVERYBODY WANTED TO SEE 'EM.

INTERVIEW PEOPLE AND FANS AND RECORD LABEL GUYS.
I DIDN'T KNOW WHO TO LET BY. SUNNY SAID NOBODY, BUT IS THAT NOBODY NOBODY, OR JUST NO NOBODIES?
THERE ARE DIFFERENT KINDS OF NOBODY.
everybody's nobody.
curio was nobody.

WELL *YES*, I KNOW THAT *NOW*.
BUT SHE WAS *INSISTENT*.
AND **SHRILL**.
I THINK I CAN PICTURE THAT.
SHE SAID SHE KNEW THE BAND.
SHE SAID SHE **ALWAYS** GOT INTO THE GREEN ROOM.
I DIDN'T *KNOW*.
SHE WAS *REALLY* MAD. LIKE I WAS MESSING EVERYTHING UP.
AND THEN **MOZE** SAW.
HE **SWORE** SHE WAS *OKAY*.
SO EVEN IF I COULD SAY NO *BEFORE*.
AND THEN THEY WERE LOCKED IN THE **WASHROOM**.
BEING HORRIBLE.

OH MY GOD THERE WAS JUST ABSOLUTELY NO EXCUSE AT ALL.
THERE WERE NOISES.
I DO NOT CARE HOW DISTANT A PERSON'S SOBRIETY MAY BE.
IT IS THEIR DUTY TO EXERCISE SUBTLETY DURING FITS OF SEXUAL INCONTINENCE.
snnk.
MOZE AND CURIO?
MOZE AND CURIO?
SERIOUSLY?
MOZE AND ANY WOMAN THAT WILL LIE STILL LONG ENOUGH.
THE MAN IS AFFLICTED, BENJAMIN.
HE'S A LIABILITY. HE WAS PART OF THE REASON I WAS EVEN THERE.
SURE WOULDA BEEN NICE IF SOMEONE HAD TOLD ME THAT.
WOW.
25% A.B.V.
THAT WAS THE FIRST JOB I WAS EVER FIRED FROM.

I GUESS I COULD BE MAD ABOUT IT.
BUT THEY DIDN'T **MEAN** FOR THAT TO HAPPEN. THEY'RE NOT **BAD PEOPLE**.
I DON'T THINK *ANYONE'S* REALLY **BAD**.
JUST, UHM.
IMPULSIVE?
SUSCEPTIBLE TO **DESIRE**.

UH-HUH.
I ABSOLUTELY, *COMPLETELY* BELIEVE CURIO WILL BE A ***REALLY GREAT PERSON*** IN A FEW YEARS.
KEEP

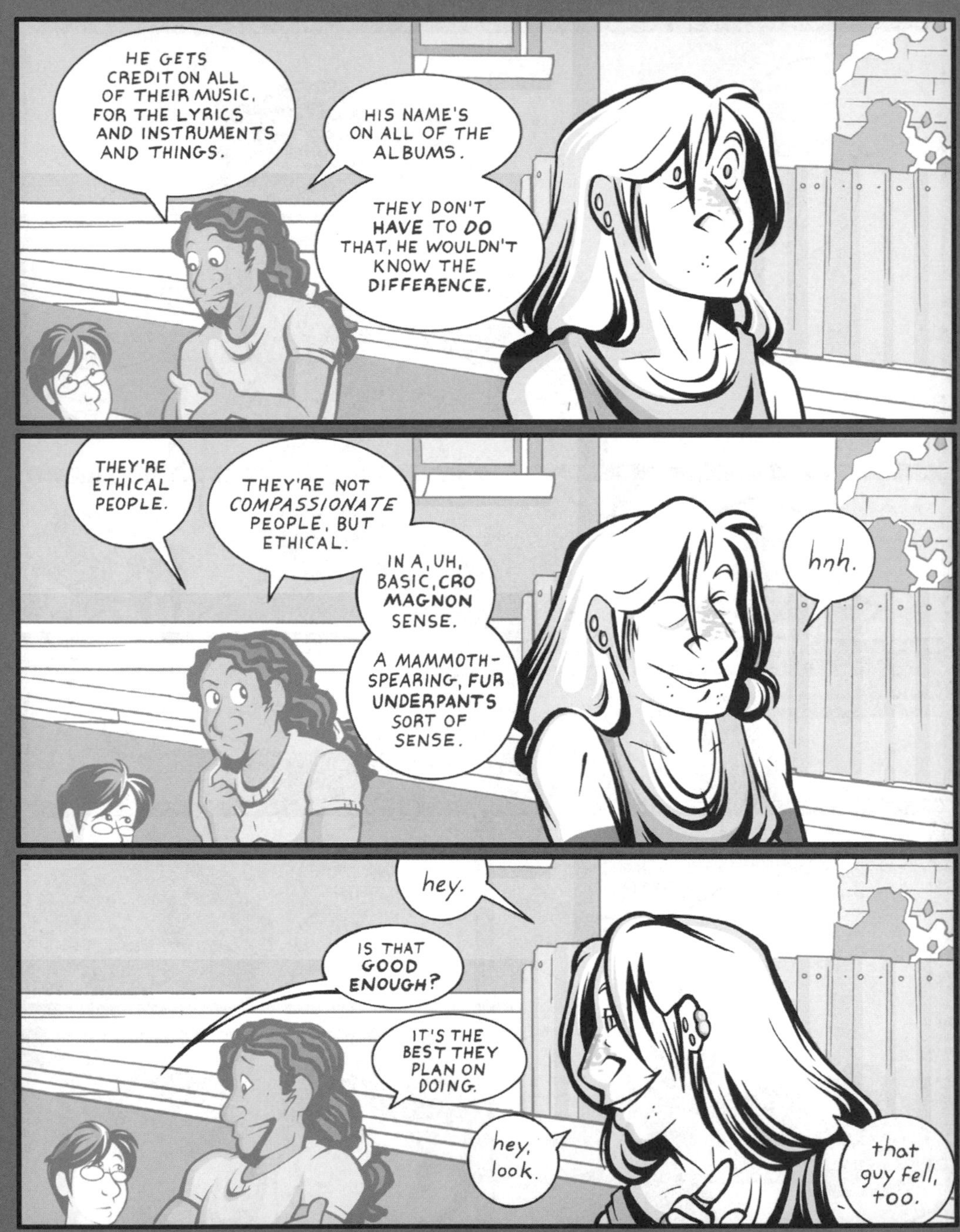
HE GETS CREDIT ON ALL OF THEIR MUSIC. FOR THE LYRICS AND INSTRUMENTS AND THINGS.
HIS NAME'S ON ALL OF THE ALBUMS.
THEY DON'T **HAVE** TO ***DO*** THAT, HE WOULDN'T KNOW THE **DIFFERENCE**.
THEY'RE ETHICAL PEOPLE.
THEY'RE NOT *COMPASSIONATE* PEOPLE, BUT ETHICAL.
IN A, UH, BASIC, CRO **MAGNON** SENSE.
A *MAMMOTH-SPEARING*, FUR **UNDERPANTS** SORT OF SENSE.
hnh.
hey.
IS THAT **GOOD ENOUGH?**
IT'S THE BEST THEY PLAN ON DOING.
hey, look.
that guy fell, too.

WHAT?
WHO FELL?
see?
he's lying down.

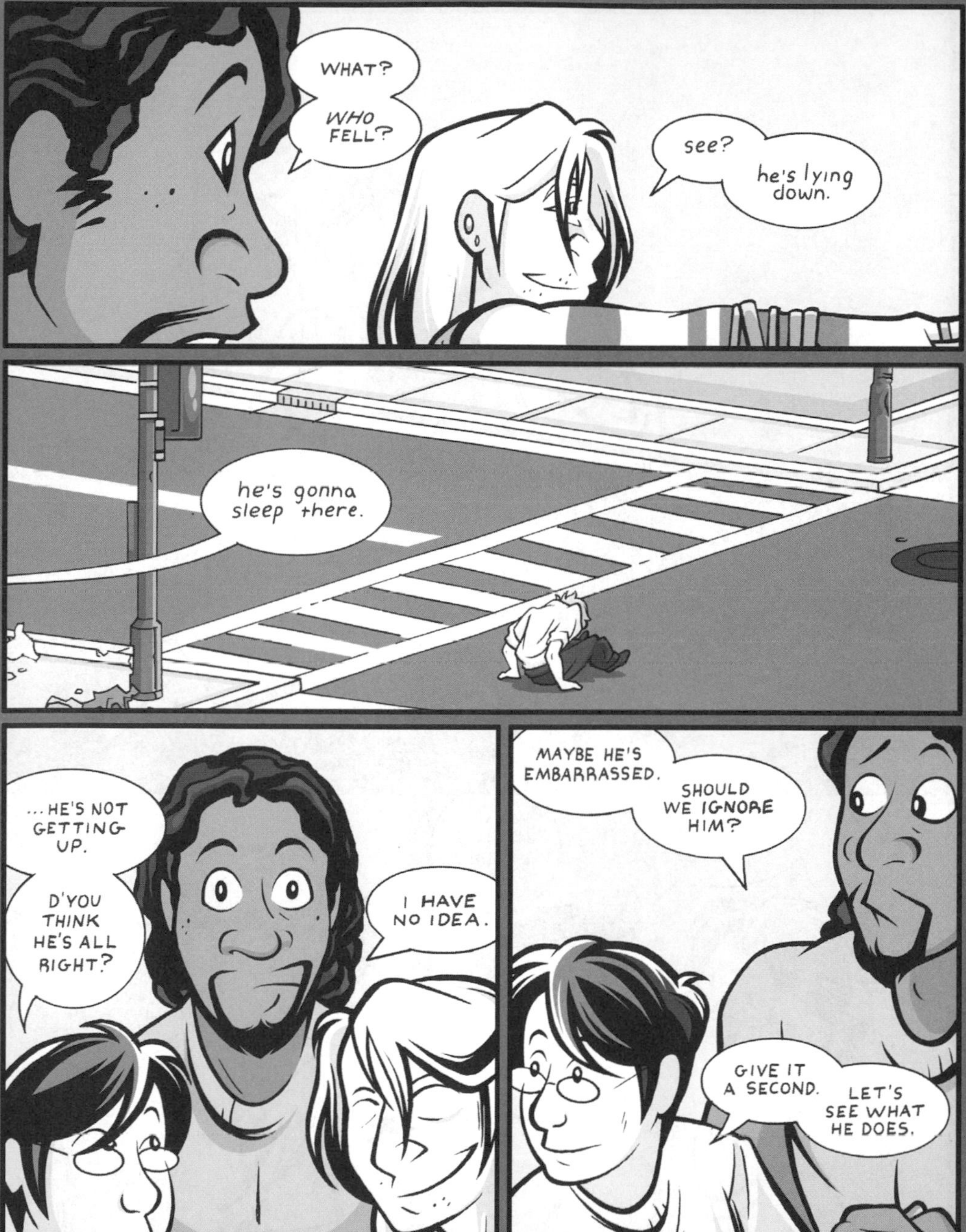

he's gonna sleep there.

...HE'S NOT GETTING UP.
D'YOU THINK HE'S ALL RIGHT?
I HAVE NO IDEA.

MAYBE HE'S EMBARRASSED.
SHOULD WE IGNORE HIM?
GIVE IT A SECOND.
LET'S SEE WHAT HE DOES.

HUH.
HE IS SERIOUSLY NOT MOVING AT ALL.
MAYBE HE'S SICK.

D'YOU REALLY THINK SO?
THEN WE OUGHTA CALL SOMEONE!
WOULD THAT MAKE HIM MAD, THOUGH?
IT WOULD BE SO INTRUSIVE.
BUT WE'RE STILL IN SKINNER. AN AMBULANCE MIGHT NOT EVEN COME HERE.
THAT HAPPENS!
CAN YOU SEE HIS FACE? IS HE ANGRY?
EXCUSE ME.

YES.
ARE YOU OKAY?
YES.
OH.
CUZ YOU'VE BEEN SITTING HERE FOR A WHILE.
YES.
BUT YOU'RE FINE.
YES.

UHM.
WOULD YOU LIKE SOME HELP?
YES.
OH MY GOD.
WE KNOW THIS GUY.

THIS IS SCREAMING GUY!
HE LIVES IN OUR BUILDING!
HEY, GENE!! SCREAMING GUY!
"SCREAMING GUY?" WHAT'S HIS REAL NAME?
HOLD ON...
OH JEEZ, I HAVE NO IDEA. HE NEVER TALKED TO ANYONE. HE JUST SCREAMED.
IS THAT YOUR BELT IN THE STORM DRAIN?
DID YOU TAKE YOUR BELT OFF?
NOT AT US, THOUGH, AT THE MOVERS. AND THE SUPER. HE SHOWED UP ABOUT SIX MONTHS AGO, WITH A MILLION BOXES.
CAN YOU KEEP HIM ON HIS FEET?
OH, ABSOLUTELY! GOD, HE SMELLS LIKE A BAR ROOM FLOOR, DOESN'T HE?
BUT DRUNK IS GOOD. DRUNK IS EASY. DRUNK I CAN HANDLE.

HE'S DRUNK?
YOU CAN'T *TELL?*
THIS MAN IS POSITIVELY FLAMMABLE.
I'VE NEVER SEEN A DRUNK PERSON, BEFORE.
NOT IN REAL LIFE.
WOAH.
tth.
...BUT I GUESS THAT'S JUST THE SUBURBS, HUH?
NO.
I THINK THAT'S MOSTLY JUST ME.
SO WHAT, DID YOU THINK HE WAS HAVING A STROKE OR SOMETHING?
CUZ I WAS AFRAID HE MIGHT BE A CRAZY PERSON.
A LOT OF THINGS COULD'VE BEEN WRONG.
he's rich.

OH. OH, GENE.
PLEASE DON'T DO THAT.
PLEASE PLEASE *PLEASE*.
it's a crime.
EXACTLY, YES.
cuz it's not mine.
WAIT, *WHAT?*
YOU DIDN'T— HE DIDN'T—
YES, HE DID.
JUST *NOW*.?
UH-HUH.
...
HEY, DO MINE!
nuh-uh.
s'got rules.
BEN!!
I KNOW, *I KNOW!*
I'M SORRY, I'M IMPRESSED! I CAN'T HELP IT!
I DIDN'T EVEN SEE HIM COME OVER HERE!
THAT WAS *AMAZING!*
drunk men only. unnumbered only.
catalyze decomposition.
this is him.

"DOCTOR ELIJAH BREWSTER BASH."
HEY, ARE YOU SURE THIS IS YOUR SCREAMING GUY? CUZ THIS ISN'T OUR BUILDING'S ADDRESS.
PRETTY *DARN* SURE. HERE, LEMME SEE.

WOW.
COURT OF JACOPA.
THAT'S WAY OVER IN THE SORROWS.

... THE *SORROWS?*
HEH. YEAH. I FORGET HOW WEIRD THAT SOUNDS WHEN WHEN YOU'RE NOT USED TO IT.
THAT'S ON THE FAR END OF KING STREET. *MANSIONS* AND STUFF.
RICH PEOPLE.
I'VE WORKED A FEW PARTIES, THERE.
JACOPA'S KINDA MID-LEVEL, LOTS OF SUIT-AND-TIE GUYS.
NUH.

HEY, DOCTOR BASH?
MN.
ELIJAH?
ELIJAH, WHERE DO YOU LIVE?

"LIVE."
HAH.

HMN.
OKAY.
NOT REALLY SURE HOW TO *INTERPRET* THAT.
DOCTOR BASH, WOULD YOU LIKE TO *GO HOME?*
WE CAN TAKE YOU HOME **RIGHT** NOW.
GO HOME WIV **YOU**.
NOW.
UH-HUH!

OH GOD.
YEZ.
YES.
HOME WIV **YOU.**
YES.
PFTT.

CRUMPLE.

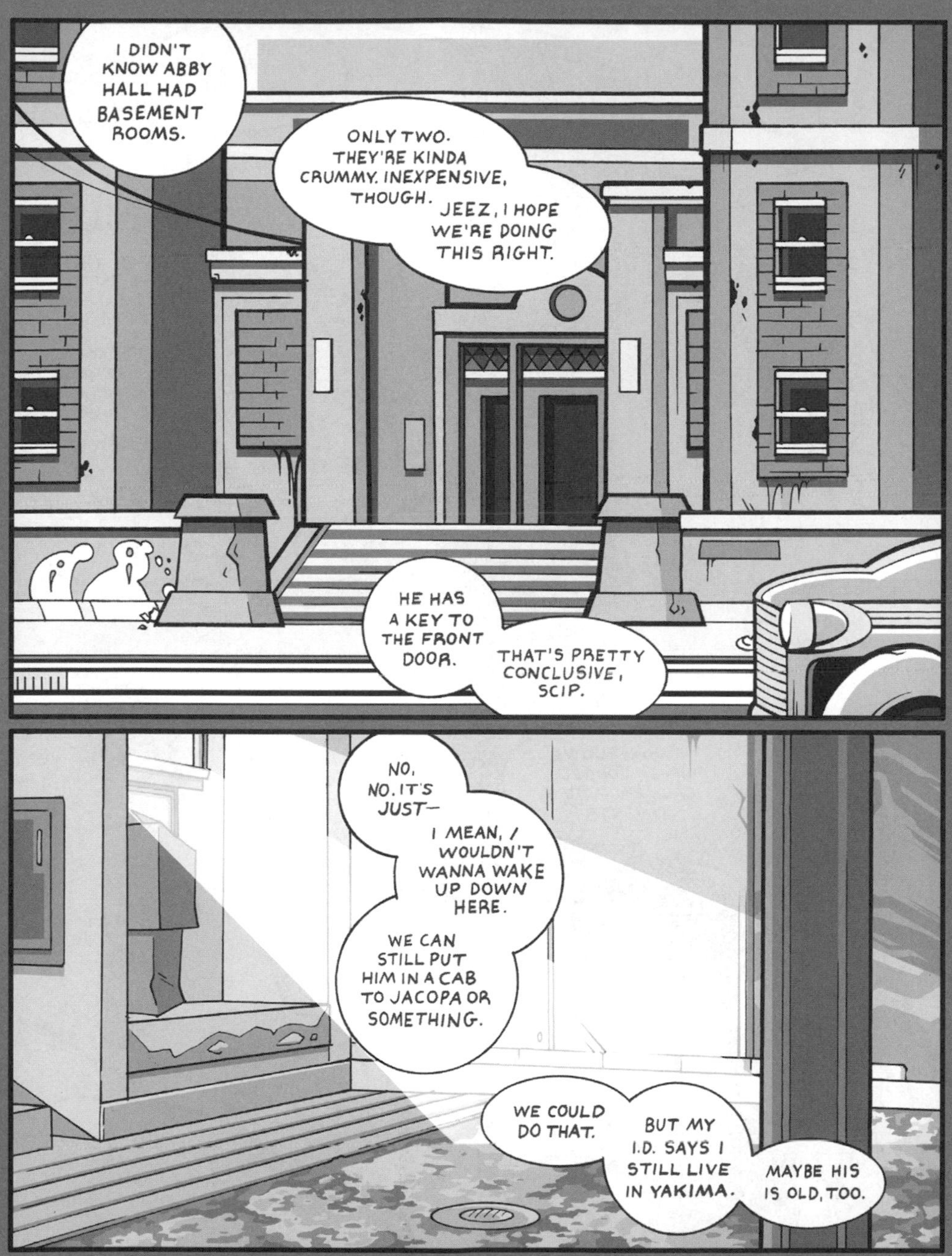
I DIDN'T KNOW ABBY HALL HAD BASEMENT ROOMS.
ONLY TWO. THEY'RE KINDA CRUMMY. INEXPENSIVE, THOUGH.
JEEZ, I HOPE WE'RE DOING THIS RIGHT.
HE HAS A KEY TO THE FRONT DOOR.
THAT'S PRETTY CONCLUSIVE, SCIP.
NO. NO. IT'S JUST—
I MEAN, I WOULDN'T WANNA WAKE UP DOWN HERE.
WE CAN STILL PUT HIM IN A CAB TO JACOPA OR SOMETHING.
WE COULD DO THAT.
BUT MY I.D. SAYS I STILL LIVE IN YAKIMA.
MAYBE HIS IS OLD, TOO.

I GUESS.
HE WAS POINTED IN THIS DIRECTION.
HE WAS ON HIS WAY *HERE*.
wWh.
MAYBE THIS IS HIS PRIVATE PLACE AWAY FROM HIS FAMILY.
A DOCTOR COULD AFFORD SOMETHING LIKE THAT.

WHO *HIDES* FROM THEIR *FAMILY*?
EVERYONE.
C'MON, YOU'VE NEVER DODGED A CALL FROM YOUR PARENTS?

IT'S JUST ME AND MY MOM.
AND NO, I DON'T DO THAT.
NEVER. *EVER.*
whait.
WHY WOULDN'T I WANT TO TALK TO MY MOM? SHE'S MY *MOM*.

WOW.
I DO NOT HAVE AN ANSWER FOR THAT.
wait. WAIT.
HM?
WAIT.

ARE YOU A BLACK MAN?
I SURE AM!

THASS FINE.
GLAD TO HEAR IT!
UH.
GOT THE DOOR OPEN.

KINDA DARK IN THERE.
YEAH, WE'RE UNDERGROUND.
TH' WINDOWS ARE ALL REALLY TINY.
FEEL FOR A SWITCH.
SNAP.
FRAGILE
... IS THIS THE STORAGE ROOM?
NO.
WE'RE IN AN APARTMENT. TH' DOOR'S GOT A PEEPHOLE.
WEIRD.
WHY HASN'T HE UNPACKED YET?
HE'S BEEN HERE FOREVER.
I DUNNO. I'M NOT SEEING ANY FURNITURE FOR THIS STUFF TO GO IN.

THERE'S A FUTON IN THE BACK, HERE.
ARE ANY OF THESE EVEN *OPEN*?
LOOK, DOCTOR BASH! IT'S YOUR COUCH!
WOULD YOU LIKE TO SIT DOWN?
DAD'S WAX
oh.
YES. Good.
YOU CAN **LIE** DOWN, IF YOU WANT.
THASS GOOD.
I WAN' THAT.
GREAT. OKAY.
OH-KAY. G'NIGHT, DOCTOR BASH.
good.

HA.
WHATTA FUNNY OL' GUY.
Y'KNOW, I DON'T THINK I COULD GO TO A "DOCTOR BASH."
BUT I WOULD WATCH A MOVIE ABOUOH.
OH OH OH.
OOOAHW MY GOD.
YEAH.
IT'S, UHM.
IT'S REALLY GOOD, ACTUALLY.
LIKE, WELL-EXECUTED.
OH MY GOD.
BEN. SERIOUSLY.
WHAT IS THAT BECAUSE OH MY FUCKING GOD.
TERTIARY SYPHILIS.
SEE? IT'S GOT A LABEL.

SYPHILIS CAN DO THIS?
UHH,
YES?
I THINK IT USED TO. THIS LOOKS PRETTY OLD.
YEAH, SEE THE TAG ON THE BACK? "1887."
HUHN.
IT WAS PACKED REALLY CAREFULLY, TOO.
THERE'S SORT OF A FOAM CRADLE IN HERE.
... MAYBE I SHOULDN'T BE TOUCHING THIS.
I ABSOLUTELY AGREE. CAN WE PUT IT AWAY, PLEASE?
OH, GOD.
IS THAT WHAT'S IN ALL OF THESE BOXES?
A HUNDRED DISEASED FACES?
no.
this is a jar.
RADIUM WATER

...
I'M GOING.
YEAH.
YOU CAN STAY. BUT I'M GONNA GO.
NO, NO. I'M COMING.
got words on it.
GENE? WE HAVE TO GO NOW.
D'YOU THINK HE'LL BE OKAY?
NO, I DO NOT THINK THAT AT ALL.
hmn.
HAN WIT CAR
I DON'T THINK DOCTOR BASH HAS BEEN OKAY IN A VERY, VERY, VERY LONG TIME.
DO I THINK HE'LL BE OKAY. HERE IN THE BASEMENT.
WITH THE DEAD FACES.
AND THE RADIATION.
NO.
I DON'T THINK HE WILL BE OKAY.
snx.

OH MY GOD.
THIS IS POSITIVELY SYMPTOMATIC.
THIS IS MORBID.
i have bugs on me.
UH.
LOOK, I'M SURE THIS STUFF IS PROBABLY SAFE.
IT WOULD HAVE TO BE.
SCARIFICATORS
HE'S LIVING WITH IT. RIGHT?
IT'S NOT THE STUFF, IT'S THE GUY WHO WANTS IT.
NO WONDER HE'S DOWN HERE, I BET HALF OF JACOPA STORMED HIS HOUSE WITH PITCHFORKS AND TORCHES.
I'M COMING BACK TOMORROW T'CHECK ON HIM. Y'WANT ME TO ASK?
GOD DON'T MENTION ME!
HA.
OH.
OH.
WHAT?
OH, BOY.
WAIT WAIT WAIT DON'T LOCK IT.
IS IT LOCKED?
m?
CLIC,
IT'S LOCKED, ISN'T IT?

AWH.
EVERYONE'S DOOR WORKS BUT MINE.
WHAT IS IT?
CLIC- CLIC CLACK.
I JUST KINDA LEFT HIS KEYS WHEREVER. I WANTED TO PUT 'EM BACK IN HIS POCKET.
Y'THINK WE COULD GET THE SUPER TO OPEN THE DOOR FOR US?
FURTHER INVOLVING ANTHONY IN THE CONTINUING MISADVENTURES OF SCREAMING GUY IS THE ONLY THING THAT COULD POSSIBLY MAKE THIS WORSE.
here.
you do th' lock with it.
c'n make it open.
MIDAS
ELIJAH B BASH
...HM.

I'LL ADMIT IT.
I LIKE THIS A LOT LESS THE SECOND TIME.
GENE, WHEN WE GAVE DOCTOR BASH BACK HIS WALLET, WE WANTED HIM TO *KEEP* IT.
yeah.
he keeps that. I keep this.
D-
DID YOU KEEP ANYTHING ELSE?
uhh.
IT'S OKAY, IT'S - THIS ISN'T *REALLY* BAD.
WE CAN GIVE EVERYTHING BACK.
AND WE WILL.
SOON.
CAN YOU DO IT? *PLEASE?*
YOU WANNA SEE HIM AGAIN ANYWAY.
OH I DID *NOT* KNOW HE WAS *KEEPING* STUFF.
I, UH.
HE'LL BELIEVE YOU. YOU'RE *GOOD* WITH LUNATICS.
WHAT DOES *THAT* MEAN?

OKAY, REAGAN?
OH.
REAGAN LOVES YOU. SHE HAS BEEN LOVING YOU.
CURIO AND THAT WEIRD GIRL WHO GETS NAKED ON TV?
THEY LOVE YOU.
WELL, I DUNNO IF -
AND SUNNY?
SUNNY, FOR GOD'S SAKE?!
OH, THAT DOESN'T COUNT, HE'S GOT THE WRONG -
BEN, YOU HAD A TERRORIST IN YOUR BEDROOM THIS MORNING.
HE DIDN'T KILL YOU. HE DIDN'T EVEN TRY.
SCRATCH SCRATCH.
Y'KNOW, YOU WOULD UNDERSTAND THAT WASN'T A BIG DEAL IF -

NO, I *WOULDN'T!* I DON'T UNDERSTAND IT AT ALL!
THAT'S THE *POINT!*
OKAY, OKAY.
YOU'RE COMPLETELY *WRONG*, BUT OKAY.
I'M DOING IT, SEE?
NOT A PROBLEM. *EASY.*
HOPE YOU DON'T COME BACK WITH ANY PARTS MISSING.
I CAN'T BELIEVE YOU'RE REALLY THIS WEIRD ABOUT DOCTOR BASH.
YES, I FIND THE STRANGE MAN IN THE BASEMENT STOCKPILING **DEATH JUNK** A LITTLE BIT APPALLING.
I CAN'T BELIEVE YOU *DON'T.*
NAH.
NO REASON TO. HE'S HAPPY DOWN HERE.
HAPPIER THAN HE WAS IN JACOPA.

SO HAPPY HE GOT DRUNK AND WENT OUT TO LIE IN AN INTERSECTION?
EVERYBODY DOES DUMB STUFF.
IT DOESN'T HAVE TO MEAN ANYTHING.
FIN.

INTERMISSION: MEET THE ELLIOTTS.

TWO PHOTOGRAPHS. COLOR. ONE OF WOMAN, NUDE. ONE OF SUBJECT IN EARLY MODEL CAR. FADED.
CHECK.
ARE YOU FROM TEMPLAR? **NO.** OF **COURSE** NOT. D'YOU KNOW WHO THAT IS OUT FRONT? THE STATUE?
THAT IS *DOVE.*
MISS DOVE, *MA* DOVE, ETCETERA. DO YOU KNOW HER? YOU DON'T?
NO, YOU DON'T. YOU DON'T KNOW HER.
SHE'S GOT A **HOLIDAY**, BUT *FINE*, WHATEVER. YOU DON'T KNOW.
ONE PAPERBACK COPY, "HERMETIC: THE PHILOSOPHY OF ISOLATION." USED.
CHECK.

SHAG-HAI
SHE WAS A MADAM. THE MADAM.
AND HER STATUE'S HOLDING A PISTOL AND A CLIENT BOOK.
IT'S SYMBOLIC.
CUZ THAT WAS HER ANGLE IN THE GAME, SHE KEPT HER WHORES SAFE AND PAID.
WHOLE OF OARLOCK LEARNED A LESSON FROM THAT.
PERFECT EXAMPLE: THIS TOWN USED TO STRADDLE TWO COUNTIES. DOVE WOULD KEEP A HOUSE IN BOTH.
NOW, WHY WOULD SHE DO THAT? CAN YOU GUESS? WANNA TRY?
CLOTHING.
SWEATERS, FIVE, ALL BLACK. OVERALLS, BLACK. THREE PAIRS, Y-FRONT UNDERPANTS.
HEAVY SOIL.
CHECK.

DIDN'T THINK SO.
SHE WOULD SWITCH UP WHEN THE LAW MADE TROUBLE.
CHANGE JURISDICTIONS.
DROP A POSSE JUST CROSSING TH' RIVER.
Y'THINK THAT'S SMART? WOULD YOU HAVE THOUGHT OF THAT?

THE OARLOCK'S ALWAYS BEEN HERE, BUT OARLOCK *NORTH*, THAT WAS ALL DOVE.
SHE *STARTED* THAT.
IT'S GALLERIES AN' ART FAGS NOW, BUT THOSE WERE BROTHELS.
SHERIFFS COULDN'T DEAL. NONE OF 'EM EVER BROUGHT IN DOVE.
AND SHE TAUGHT THIS TOWN'S WHORES HOW T'HOLD ON T'WHAT'S THEIRS.

AN'NOW HERE YOU ARE.
RECLAMATION.
SQUATTIN' IN TH' HEART OF TH' OARLOCK.
TOILETRIES. VARIOUS. USED.

HMN.
THERE'S NO RECORD OF ANY TOOTHPASTE ON YOUR ORIGINAL INTAKE MANIFEST.
YOU'LL HAVE TO PRODUCE A RECEIPT OR SURRENDER UNDOCUM-
OH FOR TH' LOVE OF—
OKAY, Y'KNOW WHAT? I'M *HAPPY.* I AM **GLAD** THIS IS **HAPPENING.**

B'DAM.
PLEASE KICK ME OUT. **PLEASE.**
YOU EARN THOSE PATS ON TH' HEAD WHILE YOU *CAN,* JUNIOR, CUZ WHEN YOU **LITTLE SHITS** FILE FOR TH' *SQUATTER'S* DEED ON THIS PLACE?
EVERY WHORE FOR **TEN SOLID BLOCKS** IS GONNA **LAWYER UP** AND *BUG-BOMB* THIS **ROACH HOLE.**

THEY ARE **LEGAL.** YOU ARE **NOT.**
YES WE ARE.
NO, YOU ARE *NOT!* YOU ARE *NOT!*
JOHN'S **FUCKED** UP THIS TIME, AN' YOU'RE ALL GONNA *KNOW IT!*

YOU THINK YOU'RE GONNA WIN THIS ONE?
BARNEY'S BORN-AGAIN COMMIES VERSUS EVERY MILLION-DOLLAR CATHOUSE IN TOWN?
AND FOR COVER YOU GOT WHAT, SOME MIGRANT WORKER PROTECTION STATUTE FROM 1920?
BULLSHIT. BULL-FUCKIN'-SHIT.
THIS FUCKIN' FARCE IS ONE NEW YORK JEW AWAY FROM COMPLETE GOD DAMNED NULLIFICATION.
YOU THINK I'M KIDDIN?
HUH?
WHUMP.
DO YOU KNOW HOW JOHN LOST HIS HAND?
SHUT UP.
I DO.
...WORKS.
WHUH?
WORKS, GIL.
TWO NEEDLES. TWO HANDMADE PAPER ENVELOPES, SMALL.
OH, HONESTLY. HONESTLY.
ONE SOUP SPOON, THREE SQUARES COTTON, SHOELACE.
USED.
"WORKS." HONESTLY.

Y'HEAR THAT, KIDS?
BETTER TOTALLY DISREGARD EVERY INTELLIGENT THING I'VE EVER SAID!
HEROIN DEPENDENCY OBVIOUSLY MAKES ME COMPLETELY INCAPABLE OF CONCLUDING THE OBVIOUS!
CRACK.
JESUS!
GET IT BACK IN THE BAG.!
Y'WANNA CHECK TH' FUCKIN' MANIFEST FOR DOPE, GIL?
WHAM
WHAM
ELLIOTT BIGELOW, YOUR PROVIDED PLACE IN "THE CIRCASSIAN," RECLAIMED BY SOVIET SEVENTEEN, IS REVOKED.
THE CHARGE OF COMMUNICABLE DEGENERACY IS DEEMED VALID.
OH, SPARE ME YOUR PROGRAMMED ADOLESCENT OUTRAGE.
CIRCUMSTANCES UNCOVERED DURING EJECTION HAVE VOIDED YOUR RIGHT OF AUTOMATIC APPEAL TO—
HEY HEY HEY,
"UNCOVERED" MY ASS. IF I DIDN'T WANT YOU FINDING THAT, IT WOULDN'T HAVE BEEN FOUND.
YOU EVER THINK OF THAT?
HUH?
FUCKIN' KIDS. DON'T KNOW A GOD DAMNED THING.
AN' WHAT'S DOWN TH' LINE FOR THIS MONKEY HOUSE IS GONNA MAKE THAT POP IN TH' FACE TH' COOKS GAVE YOU FEEL LIKE A LOVE TAP, SWEETHEART.

FFF—! ASSHOLE!
OUT.
GET HIM OUT.
AND YOUR FRIEND IS GONNA PAY FOR WHATEVER HE'S BUSTING UP BACK THERE, BIGGS.
HA!
WITH WHAT? IDIOT.
HEY.
HEY
DON'T YOU FUCKIN' MANHANDLE ME, YOU—
JESUS CHRIST, FORGET HIM AND HELP ME!
THE STUPID ONE STARTED A FIRE!

GET UP.
LIL' GOOSE-STEPPERS'LL BE BACK FOR YA TH' SECOND THEY GET TH' SMOKE CLEARED.
FUCK YOU.

ARE YOU CRYING?
NO.
BECAUSE THAT'S FINE. I DON'T CARE IF YOU CRY, EJ. YOUR EMOTIONAL INSTABILITY IS JUST PART OF TH' SCENERY, NOW.
SHUT UP.

EVERYBODY FUCKIN' HATES ME.
OH, HELL.
HEY, CAN WE DO THIS WALKIN'?
WE'RE BREAKIN' CURFEW.

THAT FUCKIN' FIASCO RECLAMATION HAD DOWNTOWN MAKES WHORESVILLE A NO-GO ZONE 'TIL DAWN.
GOTTA GET OVER T'SKINNER OR SUMTHIN.'
I DON'T EVER EVEN HAVE ANY THING THAT'S MINE.
YOU GOT T'KEEP YOUR JACKET.

JESUS.
BARNEY JOHN.
I DID TIME WITH THAT GUY.
FW
FIN.

Footnotes.

Page 1

Curio and Tuesday aren't really friends. They're two people from similar backgrounds who frequent the same social circles and value the same things, so they inevitably see a lot of one another without ever planning to. Their relationship consists of very little besides subtle one-upmanship and criticizing one another.

This isn't a uniquely female kind of interaction, but I see it a lot with insecure women and girls; the sort of people who loudly declare themselves best friends forever, and then sever all ties over basically nothing . . . only to make up the moment one of them has something to boast about.

By the way, I feel I have to apologize to horologists everywhere for misusing the title of their field of study. In the real world, horology concerns the art and science of time, and timekeeping technology. In Templar, it's a flaky pseudoscience, comparable to astrology. Sorry, clock fans.

Page 2

Shiner brand make-up. Model a split lip, dab on some bruises! Because you're hurting, missy, and you should damn well *look* the part.

I can very easily imagine sullen, sheltered teenagers plastering this stuff on an inch thick before hitting the clubs. Extravagant claims of psychological trauma are routinely substituted for personal depth. Is trumped-up physical trauma really that much of a stretch?

Page 4

Tuesday is considerably more clever than Curio, so when the claws come out, it's over before it starts. She'll dredge up something personal you told her a year ago, mix it with a little armchair psychology, and then piss on you for getting mad in the first place. A very effective mix of techniques.

Page 6

Not a great segue. If I had it to do over again, Tuesday's word balloons would be coming from Curio's penthouse apartment, which I would have put in the background. But eh, whatta ya gonna do.

Anyway... Enter Reclamation. Sort of a combination of European-style squatting, revolutionary communism, blue-collar unions, and cult of personality, featuring one Barnabas John.

Every once in a while, someone will write me to say they think Reclamation is a great concept. Those people are scary. Rec is aggressive, idealist, and quasi-militant. Organizations like that? They start wars.

The medal on the leftmost figure is a reference to "Bread and Roses," a strike slogan generally interpreted to mean that bare sustenance (bread) isn't enough, and the working class deserves enough pay and benefits from their employers to live with dignity (roses).

Page 8

Barnabas John. I love him; he is just so bulldog ugly. Ugly people are fun to draw.

In this instance, "John" is actually a Navajo surname. Back when America's native population was being converted, in Templar's continuity as well as our own, the priests and missionaries ran out of Christian surnames before they ran out of Indians. So, they began using first names for last names. It's likely that John is part native, although how much doesn't really matter.

His prosthetic hand caused a lot of confusion with readers. Some people thought it was futuristic-looking. The exact opposite is true: it's wretchedly primitive, something an American Civil War veteran might have worn. The prosthetic I used for reference was so old that it was black with patina.

Page 10

Numbers is an okay kid. I like Numbers. But she's kind of on the fast track to jarring disappointment.

She's named for the Book of Numbers, found in the Christian Old Testament, the Hebrew Bible, and the Torah. Her parents are probably census-takers or accountants or something.

Page 13

I have no idea what's in these bottles. Possibly homebrew tear gas. Possibly harmless vapors with impressive, billowy visuals that don't do anything.

Two stable liquids are isolated in two separate glass bottles, which are taped together. When the bottles smash and the liquids mix: wholesale panic.

I imagine the effect is especially satisfying when the target has no idea what you just hit them with.

Page 15

The Cook Family, indeed. Why "The Cook Family?" I'll tell you later, but some of you have already guessed.

Cooks aren't making a statement or attempting to draw attention to a pet cause. They're not specifically anti-Reclamation, either. They're just dicks. Real-life griefers, ruining your day for the sheer pleasure of watching you suffer.

They're a routine nuisance. The riot cops are probably there in anticipation of Cooks, rather than rowdy Reclamation adherents. Not that they'll ever admit the Cooks exist.

I stole this flaming gas canister attack from

a photo I saw of a South Korean protester pulling a similar stunt.

Page 16

The riot cop's gun – a paintball-firing model designed for crowd control – is apparently so distinctive that at least one reader identified the reference I used for it immediately. He also informed me the cop was holding the gun wrong, which demonstrates how much I know about firearms. I fixed that mistake for print.

Page 18

Claudius R. Graves, previously glimpsed on a billboard in the first book, hosts his terrible, terrible show.

Claudius is wearing a *toga praetexta*, which is distinguished by its crimson (or according to some sources, purple) stripe. This Roman toga was reserved for kings, magistrates, and selected priests, and was occasionally bestowed as an honor independent of formal rank. I guess Claudius thinks quite a lot of himself. And he probably has some very creepy political views swirling around in that laurel-crowned, retrophilic head of his.

He's not technically a Pastime, since he's wearing a suit and using modern technology. But if he ran into one from his favorite era of Roman history, they probably wouldn't disagree on much.

And "Treasure" is yet another entry for the "I thought I made that up!" list, a very recent addition. I just saw a kid with that name in a documentary about child beauty pageants.

Page 20

Now playing on the laptop: *Sky Vikings and the Thunderbird Tribe*. No more violent than most *Looney Tunes* cartoons, really.

Page 22

Dude is exaggerating. The two-story drop wouldn't kill him. He wouldn't *enjoy* it, but it wouldn't *kill* him. Unless he landed on his head or something.

Page 23

Useless detail time.

Ben lives on Pakhom Way in the firmly lower-middle-class neighborhood of Riverside. This is a contraction of the street's real name, which is "The Street of the Way in the Spirit of Our Father Saint Pachomius of God."

Saint Pachomius was an Egyptian monk and a Christian hermit, famous for developing the concept of cenobitic monasticism. Before Pakhom was the age of "The Desert Fathers," where holy men and women lived alone in the barren places instead of congregating and living communally. Pakhom Way was named by the founding inhabitants of Templar – a band of idealistic Jesuit troublemakers – in the hopes that it would remind their Indian converts to lead holy and harmonious lives as they left their towns and villages and came to live as Christians among the white men.

Pakhom is one of the oldest streets in Templar, and it's seen everything from farmland to posh uptown luxury to decay to renewal. If an empty lot zoned to turn into a new parking garage turns out to be a 150-year-old slave cemetery, or the basement of a building is built over the foundations of an old adobe hut, Pakhom is probably running nearby.

Page 25

Paintball rounds meant to mark perpetrators in crowd situations are real. They exist. *Stinky* paintball rounds, I made up. I wouldn't be surprised if they became real eventually, though.

Page 26

The glass falling into the apartment instead of down onto the street from Ben's theoretically broken window would be vital. It means the cops would think "Bill" the Cook broke in from the outside, firmly placing Ben in the role of victim instead of accomplice or fugitive-harborer.

Page 28

If you're shaving your wrists, you're probably shaving just about everything else, too.

Page 29

A guy as built as Scipio being this body-shy is kind of unusual. But what can I say, it fits.

Page 33

Two more years of schooling before graduation, plus being held back a year, means Pippi's around sixteen or seventeen years old.

Page 35

Freudians, start your engines.

Page 37

Riding that adrenaline wave for all it's worth, eh Benny?

Page 40

Third panel: Reagan mentioned this statue of centaur-style Andrew Jackson in the previous book.

The city didn't just cut the heads off the statue's figures, but moved the sculpture, base and all, to a low-traffic area. This means that offended, socially progressive vandals can now deface it in near-perfect privacy.

It's etched and graffiti-covered, and it's been attacked by a mob of students from the American Indian Movement with hammers. The city fathers are loath to fix it up, though, since that would be like detailing a rusted-out AMC Gremlin you're planning on junking soon, anyway.

Page 42

I can't look at this page without picturing Scip effortlessly reducing Ben to pulp with those gigantic hands of his. He looks like he could pop Ben's head off like a cork out of a champagne bottle.

That's another one of those details that only matters to me. Scip's huge hands.

By the way, getting Scip and Ben to share the same panel is always a bit of a struggle. I cheat a lot, because the size difference between them excludes so many potential layouts. The main panel of this page is probably the most proportionally accurate to one another that I've ever drawn them.

Page 43

I wouldn't call Scip socially incompetent. More like . . . good-naturedly clueless. It honestly would not occur to him that a grown man a little over five feet, four inches tall might not want to talk about his height. ("Let's call it five-five" is code for "I am shorter than this, but not by a lot.")

Ben's not hyper-sensitive about his height. He's a lifelong runt, he's had twenty-one years to get used to it. But boy, that sure took the wind out of his sails pretty quick, didn't it? And Scip happily steamrolls right along with the conversation. The big guy doesn't even notice.

To be fair, though, Scip ducks to get through doors, breaks furniture, can't quite fit in his own bed, has trouble finding clothes... The world is, in general, just a bit too small for him. He's probably convinced that, when it comes to height, Ben got the better deal.

Page 44

Skinner. The crap part of town.

The Black Mariah Gentlewoman's Club? We'll be hearing from them.

Page 45

Kingdom Come is an "adult store." In Templar, that means it can simultaneously get you drunk, sell you a gun, and register you to vote, all in the same building. "Adult" doesn't mean "pornographic." It means "stuff you can't get ahold of until you're at least 18."

Page 47

I stole the name "Flannery" from the book *Freakonomics*, where the author has predicted it will be a popular, hip, upper-class name in 2015, a moniker that the wealthy and educated will pioneer and the unwashed masses will later scramble to adopt. (Such was the fate of names like "Britney" and "Heather," apparently.) We shall see, huh?

This does not indicate that Templar is set in 2015 or later. I just liked the name.

Page 49

Mondo films are, by popular definition, clips of humans and animals dying.

Page 51

Yep. Gordon isn't actually allowed to buy anything interesting in Kingdom Come, but he shows up anyway. And he just received a 24-hour ban from a store he never actually buys anything at.

Isn't that odd? I think it's odd.

Page 52

You know I'm writing fiction when I suggest a porn anime about a retarded sex demon wouldn't sell well.

Page 55

The Cook Family is quite possibly the only Templar subculture Reagan doesn't talk shit about. She probably interprets their actions as expressions of gloriously unfettered impulse, which she can respect.

Page 56

Simultaneously, Scipio thinks it's all nonsense, because he can't see the point in it. I mean, if it doesn't have a point, nobody would *do* it, right?

Page 58

"Funeral fetish" isn't necrophilia. It's about the ceremony, the interment, the grief, all that jazz. Necrophilia is just about the body.

I've never heard of anyone with a real funeral fetish, but if that turned out to be true, I wouldn't be surprised.

"Stump Humping" is real, but it's not called that in fetish circles. Amputee fetishism is pretty widespread and well-established.

"Chicks sitting on birthday cakes" has been identified as a reference to *Achewood*, another webcomic. But it's not. This is actually real. A woman named Ducky DooLittle, a performance artist/sexologist, used to get dressed up as "Knockers the Klown" and sit on birthday cakes in public. She claimed that it got her off.

Too strange to be fiction.

Templar's weird sex probably isn't any weirder than it is in our world, considering some websites I've seen. It's just a little more public, due to the fact that prostitution is legal there, and some of the brothels specialize in meeting esoteric needs.

Page 59

The online version of this page gets linked to a lot.

Page 60

A closer view of Loft's Wall/Loftwall, the relocated Spanish battlement.

Page 61

These two will argue about anything.

Page 65

Moze and Sunny. Gosh, do I love Moze and Sunny. Goblin, too. They're minor supporting cast in the grand scheme of things, but these two take up a lot of mental real estate when I'm dreaming up future scenes.

Page 69

Red Eric has a few facial characteristics associated with Fetal Alcohol Syndrome. Just sayin'.

His shirt's logo is strongly inspired by a fringed, faux-leather jacket a friend of mine received from an uncle for Christmas. It had "COCAINE" written across the back in rhinestones.

My friend was six at the time.

Also: Assuming Ben's unexpected morning visitor was handsome, hoping Red Eric turned out to be cute... Ray's taste in men should be pretty apparent, by now.

Page 71

Diesel is not for lightweights. It's a nasty, brutal variation of street hockey, with a touch of gladiatorial combat thrown in for color. Red Eric and the Get-Ups are participating in a form of formalized cheating that would be completely acceptable, if they hadn't been tossed out of the league.

Jumping the match won't get them back into the league. They're just being jerks and disrupting as many games as they can find. They don't always come out on top, but as long as they're giving everybody else a hard time, they're satisfied.

Page 72

Falkyn is probably a lot like an '80s hair band from our world, one of those stadium acts with the kind of sound every '80s teenager loved, but would never admit to liking now.

Page 73

If Sunny weren't a candy-sucking, foul-mouthed former delinquent, he would probably be a Fortune 500 CEO. Some people just have naturally-occurring business skills. He's one of them.

Page 77

Sunny and Moze's given names come to light. Moze doesn't much care what people call him, but Sunny's preference for his American-style nickname is something I saw a lot of from the immigrant/first generation kids I knew in school.

Page 79

A short history of Nicky Collision.

Nicky is partially inspired by Jesse Camp, the notoriously annoying and talentless winner of MTV's original "Who Wants To Be A VJ?" contest. Unlike Jesse, Nicky seems to have caught hold the very last rung of the celebrity ladder and maintained Z-list status, instead of spiraling down into obscurity.

Page 80

"Grapevine" is a reference to *Rolling Stone*. Both of those magazines are named after old Motown hits. "Sugar" is referencing *Creem*, an incredibly influential music magazine that coined the phrases "punk rock" and "heavy metal." Gracing the cover of either would require professional and personal compromises Sunny is not willing to make.

A lot of Sunny's opinions and paranoid fantasies about what it is to be in the music industry come from an article entitled "The Problem with Music," written by Steve Albini. Steve is probably best known for producing Nirvana's *In Utero*. The article goes into terrifying detail about how a freshly-signed band can make the industry roughly $3,000,000 with their first album, and still somehow find themselves $14,000 in debt to their label. Ugly stuff, and completely true. It ends with the immortal line, "Some of your friends are probably already this fucked."

Page 81

Moze was not originally conceived as a fat, hairy, ogre-like Lothario. That just happened on the page.

The secrets of his success? Casual lewdness and unswerving honesty.

Page 82

A baryton is a ridiculously difficult-to-play string instrument. A crumhorn is a woodwind, shaped like a cane. Both are unpopular antiques with very few people who play them, these days.

And telling Gene you can't play any instrument at all is like telling him your brain is broken.

Page 83

Curio's boobs are fake. Implants. That explains why she has two cantaloupe halves standing at attention in her shirt.

I was determined to show Ben sneakin' a quick peek without it coming off as sleazy or creepy on this page. It was easier than I thought it would be.

Poor guy. He's only human.

Page 85

The obvious, in plain English. Everyone gets around to asking Ben this question eventually.

Page 90

Is Tuesday taking off with half the cast in tow because she's sincerely interested in getting to know them, or because she knows that doing so will enrage Curio? Probably a little of both.

Page 93

If you ever find yourself in the presence of a person who uses the term "friend-stealer" after the age of fifteen, run. Run until you can run no longer.

Page 94

Rumor mill: Army soldiers and Special Forces guys invading and sterilizing enemy hideouts are advised by their commanders to kill any women opponents they find first, before the men. That's because any woman in a violent organization, such as a terrorist group or guerrilla squad, is probably about ten times crazier and more fucked up than any man in the room.

Enter Lavender Menace. Google their name to get an idea of their membership demographics.

Diesel only became equal opportunity among the genders recently, within the last ten years. And like lady terrorists, lady Diesel players have had to prove themselves above and beyond what's required of your average male player. So, if any teams there are gonna go after Eric, Lavender Menace will be first.

Page 101

One of my goals with Scip's personality is to reflect the influence his interest in Buddhism has had on his world view, without having him spew religious terminology and quotes every five pages. I'm slowly getting more competent in my attempts at that.

Page 103

The closest Templar will ever get to being autobiographical.

I experienced something similar to this years ago, when I helped drag a drunk, inert stranger out of the middle of the street and escort him to his apartment. This account is heavily fictionalized.

I originally intended to introduce Dr. Eli "Screaming Guy" Bash in a completely different manner, with a lot more aggression and tears. This way is much better.

Page 111

Cars are hard, for me. I'm easing myself into it. Be merciful.

Page 112

Judging by the reader response to this page when I first put it online, Scip being a momma's boy came as a surprise to no one. That means either Scip is such a well-rendered character that my readers know what would be normal for him by now, or that I'm very predictable.

Page 113

If Scip took everything a drunk said to him personally, he couldn't do his job. Drunk-wrangling is practically in a bodyguard's job description.

Page 116

This anatomical wax was referenced from a similar specimen currently housed in the Mütter Museum in Philadelphia. Visit, if you ever get a chance. It's an amazing place.

Wax anatomical models, usually featuring specific diseases and injuries, were popular teaching aids in the the times before refrigeration and advanced embalming techniques. Keeping actual corpses around for medical students to study was impractical, back then. Sure, you got your occasional hanged criminal for dissection, but they curdled pretty quickly.

Wax models eventually fell out of favor after the advent of durable and accurate plaster models. Unlike wax models, which required protective cases, plaster could be extensively handled by students and teachers.

Page 117

Not so very long ago, radiation was touted as a miracle cure-all, the same way colloidal silver and shark cartilage are sold today. Patent medicine manufacturers took a grain of truth – the fact that extremely low levels of radioactivity, in the form of naturally emanating radon gas, were common in "health springs" thought to have healing properties – and just ran with it. "Radioactive" was the "organic" of its day, and touted as imparting vigor and well-being. Radium was put into chocolate, toothpaste, contraceptives, suppositories, and beauty aids.

Special jugs were also sold to help irradiate your drinking water. That's what Gene's holding.

The doses of radiation a reasonable person could ingest from homemade irradiated water were harmless. But too much radium, taken orally, could rot your face off and turn your bones into Swiss cheese. This fate befell Eben Byers, a wealthy American socialite, athlete, and industrialist. It had happened before, but not to anyone quite so rich and important. Eben's death in 1932 brought about the end of the irradiated patent medicine boom, and the sudden empowerment of a previously toothless little government office known as the FDA.

"Alternative medicine." Gotta love it.

Page 126

A *Cliff's Notes* version of the history of the Oarlock, Templar's entirely legal brothel district.

Dove's clothes date her to the Edwardian era. I have no doubt this portrait of her is heavily idealized.

Male whores don't make up a huge percentage of the Oarlock's working population, but a representation of them was included in the memorial for the sake of being politically correct.

Page 127

We saw this lady with the forehead tattoo at the Reclamation rally. Looks like she got a little roughed up.

Page 128

Dove's strategy for keeping one step ahead of the law was a real one. It was used in Nevada before the advent of legal prostitution, and in Phenix City, Alabama. The latter was so out of control that martial law was declared and the National Guard had to be called in before its prostitution, gambling, and drug-running mobs were finally shut down in the 1950s.

Page 130

"Works" is slang for the instruments and accessories junkies require to get their fix. I thought everybody knew this term, but it caused some confusion when I originally uploaded this page.

Bigelow's works are indicative of a heroin addict. His kit sounds pretty comprehensive, so he's probably been hooked for a while. Long before he came to live at the Circassian, certainly, and these Rec kids never noticed. He's either been very careful, or these kids are very naïve.

Page 131

Circassians are a real ethnic group in the Caucasus Mountains, but this brothel's name is a reference to the phenomenon of "the Circassian beauty." Literature concerning Circassian women frequently mentioned their extreme beauty, and claimed this made them very desirable as slave concubines. Mark Twain, Don Juan, and Voltaire all mentioned Circassian beauties.

P.T. Barnum was the first American showman to capitalize on this legend and display a woman he claimed was a Circassian beauty: Zalumma Agra, in the 1860s. Her Caucasian racial purity, credited for her beauty, was strongly emphasized . . . which is pretty funny to modern sensibilities, because she sported a huge afro as part of her stage get-up. That hairstyle eventually became a trademark feature of every supposedly Circassian showgirl.

Page 133

I guess that jacket we saw in the street at the end of the second chapter didn't stay there for long.

And that's book two. Remember, there's always more at http://www.templaraz.com.

Thanks for bothering, guys.

Sketches.

LET'S PLAY SOMETHING ELSE.
PLAY-DOH VIVISECTION FUN SET
SHITLOAD
ASSEMBLY
REQUIRE

About the artist.

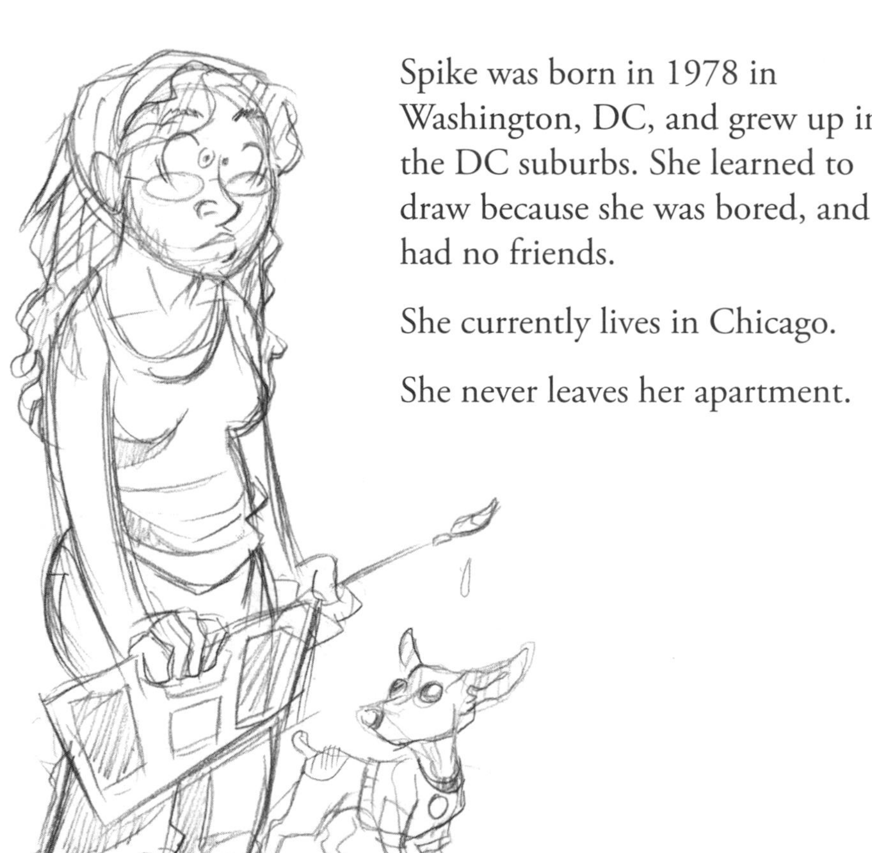

Spike was born in 1978 in Washington, DC, and grew up in the DC suburbs. She learned to draw because she was bored, and had no friends.

She currently lives in Chicago.

She never leaves her apartment.